The Alliance of the Hearts of Jesus and Mary: Hope of the World

The Alliance of the Hearts of Jesus and Mary: Hope for the World

The Alliance of the Hearts of Jesus and Mary: Hope of the World

Michael O'Carroll, C.S.Sp.

Queenship
PUBLISHING COMPANY
P.O Box 42028 Santa Barbara, CA 93140-2028
(800) 647-9882 • (805) 957-4893 • Fax: (805) 957-1631

Dedication

To the Bishops and Faithful of the Philippines, in gratitude.

Library of Congress #: 97-

Published by:
    Queenship Publishing
    P.O. Box 42028
    Santa Barbara, CA 93140-2028
    (800) 647-9882 • (805) 957-4893 • Fax: (805) 957-1631

Printed in the United States of America

ISBN: 1-882972-98-8

Contents

Photos

Cover Photo: This picture of the two Hearts was brought to Ireland from the Philippines. In a Dublin house the Hearts bled; the blood is visible and palpable. Let it stand as a symbol of the devotion of the Philippines to the Alliance of the two Hearts, publicly admitted by John Paul II, and of the profound union in this dual mystery between Ireland and the great Asian Republic, a union sealed in love, service and mutual trust.

Back Photo: This image was received in Japan from a great French missionary, F. Alain Quenouelle, of the French Missionary Society, with thirty five years service, and care of a Foyer de Charite. He guarantees its utter authenticity, universally acknowledge bisides. Let it stand as a symbol of the revival of true devotion to the Sacred Heart of Jesus within the Catholic Church worldwide.

Preface

The pages which follow are an introduction to a theme that increasingly interests and concerns committed Catholics. They have the examples of Pope John Paul II to encourage them. The title of this book comes from him. My aim has been to suggest the depths of doctrine uncovered by the revelation of the Sacred Heart of Jesus and the Immaculate Heart of Mary, while keeping my presentation accessible to the ordinary reader. There is within this reality a wealth of power and glory, for we touch the very central figures in the entire universe: God incarnate, "through whom and for whom all things were made" (Col 1:16), and the One chosen and adorned to give him his fitting place at the heart of all things.

So sublime, so mysterious, so awe-inspiring; and yet, comes within the reach of anyone with good will who has the happiness, the blessing, to believe. It is the innermost secret of the Gospel come to life; a man recently come from a village carpenter's bench, walking by a lakeside not far away, picking up some companions, with whom he would become a traveling preacher, his origin in a wayside hut, his final act that of a publicly disgraced culprit, a troublemaker for the religious establishment, crushed into oblivion.

But he was the Lord of heaven and earth, and out of his tomb came the first shining notice that he is on his way to take over and control all things. Where are those who thought to destroy, eliminate him? Down through the centuries he repeats this total reversal of worldly, purely, worldly, success.

Who really is he? Every generation must ask the question, which has an answer satisfying and yet prompting still more curiosity. The answer I offer to the reader is that of his Heart, itself more luminous through the Heart of his Mother.

Feast of the Presentation of the Lord, 2 February, 1997.
Michael O'Carroll, C.S.Sp

Abbreviations

AAS   Acta Apostolicae Sedis

D Sp   Dictionnaire de Spiritualite

EphM   Ephemerides Mariologicae

ORE   L'Osservatore Romano, English Weekly Edition

PL   Patrologia Latina

Chapter I
The Approach

(i)

It has to be personal. I grew up in the Catholic Church in which the Sacred Heart of Jesus was central, dominant, radiant. One of the earliest memories I cherish is of kneeling with my brothers and dear mother before an image of the Sacred Heart, while the parish curate, Fr. John Kelly, read the act of consecration.[1] As time passed, I lived with this idea which was an ideal. I took part in the relevant ceremonies centered on the wonderful theme, not always with any great understanding, but respectfully, assuming that this was integral to practice of the Catholic religion.

I came to know of certain events and official pronouncements. One great event was the consecration of the human race and the Church to the Sacred Heart by Pope Leo XIII on 11 June, 1899, on the eve of the second Christian millennium. We learned later that a German Good Shepherd nun living in Portugal, Sister Droesche-Vichering, had written to the Pope to inform him that such was the Lord's wish. A major official pronouncement was the Encyclical Letter, *Haurietis Aquas,* issued by Pius XII, 15 May, 1956, to clarify and fully expound the theological basis of the devotion. This was doctrinally more important than Pius XI's Encyclical *Miserentissimus Redemptor,* on reparation to the Sacred Heart of Jesus, followed by another from the same Pope, *Caritate Christi Complusi.*

Meanwhile, we knew of such valued forms of piety as the Nine Fridays; we heard of the worldwide apostolate of Fr. Matteo-Crawley on enthronement of the Sacred Heart in homes; in this he had papal approval. We knew of great church buildings raised to honor the mystery, principally the Basilica begun in Rome by St. John Bosco,

---

[1] Curate in the parish of Newcastle West, Co., Limerick; a patriot priest who enjoyed the confidence of the nationalist movement.

at the invitation of Pope Pius IX, and other world-famous at Montmartre above the city of Paris, its existence the result of a national vow, the inscription over the main entrance so moving: *Sacratissimo Cordi Jesu, Gallia grata, poenitens ac devota.*[2]

Such consciousness was given depth and security by participation in the Liturgy, at the celebration of the feast authorized in 1765, extended to the universal Church in 1856, a first class feast with octave since Pius XI.[3] This Pope had instituted the feast of the Kingship of Christ in 1925 by the Encyclical Letter *Quas Primas*; he ordered that the annual act of consecration of all to the Sacred Heart of Jesus, renewing that of Leo XIII, should be made on this feast.

These acts of liturgical and popular piety meant very much for those ordained priests in that age. The priest was celebrant of the Mass and he read the Office in his Breviary. He would be the one to read the act of consecration on behalf of the faithful. Such privileges were a challenge to his personal commitment to his membership of the Church, and to his priestly ministry. Normally he would have had no reservation, no doubt about the meaning of the liturgical and popular homage, though he might have needed some study and serious reflection on its total significance.

This duty can no longer be neglected. There has been a decline in Catholic devotion to the Sacred Heart of Jesus. It is not universal, not equally low in every place; the symptoms are not everywhere alike. It is sometimes just indifference or apathy, not always with the dismissive phrase "preconciliar piety." Encouragement from authority has not always been forthcoming or generous; directives have been lacking.

---

[2] Some of the great names of France, among them her great soldiers, were associated with the national vow; elsewhere one noted the public act of consecration of the Ecuador in 1873 by the saintly layman, Garcia Moreno, the consecration of Belgium in 1919 by Cardinal Mercier, in presence of the king and queen and parliamentary representatives: Spain, 1890; Colombia, 1900; Mexico, 1914.

[3] The delay in granting the feast does no honour to the Roman authorities; it had been requested by the Sacred Heart of St. Margaret Mary Alacoque in 1675; what delay in time here, as in other similar cases, signifies, has not been explained — because it is inexplicable.

(ii)

Is there one determining cause for this decay? In particular, is it an effect of Vatican II? The Council taught admirable truths about Jesus Christ. In clarifying the doctrine of revelation, freeing it from abstractions, the Council Fathers took a personalist as distinct from a propositional approach, that dictated by a reading of Hebrews 1:1-2: "God spoke of old to our fathers at various times and in many ways by means of the prophets. But he has at the end of these days spoken to us in his Son, whom he has appointed heir of all things, and through whom he made the world." In the Constitution on Divine Revelation, we read this paraphrase of these words: "The most intimate truth which this revelation gives us about God and the salvation of man shines forth in Christ, who is himself both the mediator and the sum total of Revelation."

Two other pithy statements on Christ will bear quoting. In dealing with the mystery of the Church, the conciliar Fathers had this to say: "The Son, accordingly, came, sent by the Father who, before the foundation of the world, chose us and predestined us in him for adoptive sonship. For it is in him that it pleased the Father to restore all things (Cf. Eph. 1:4-5 and 10). The Pastoral Constitution on the Church in the modern world addresses problems of our time, including the very meaning of man. "In reality," we read, "it is only in the mystery of the Word made flesh that the mystery of man truly becomes clear. For Adam, the first man, was a type of him who was to come. Christ, the Lord, Christ the new Adam, in the very revelation of the mystery of the Father and of his love, fully reveals man to himself and brings to light his most high calling. It is no wonder, then, that all the truths mentioned so far should find in him their source and their most perfect embodiment."

The Council did not address a problem debated by Dominicans and Franciscans, on the absolute primacy of Christ, its starting point the question whether God would have become man if Adam had not sinned. But in the whole body of teaching there is no doubt about the central, preeminent indispensable role of the God-man.

In over 100,000 words there is nothing about the Sacred Heart of Jesus; the title is not even mentioned. Is there a parallel here with the attitude taken towards St. Joseph?: total silence — his name occurs once in a quotation from what was then the Roman Canon, now Eucharistic Prayer I — his name had been inserted in the Canon by John XXIII during the first session of the Council.[4]

It will serve to pursue the parallel. The Council, pastoral and ecumenical by Pope John's decision, biblical by its choice of method, had to treat of problems to which the saint has relevance: the universal call to holiness — his holiness ranks him next to Our Lady, and was lived in a setting which could evoke widespread sympathy; the theology of work; the Church's relations with the Jewish people — he was the most important Jew of his time after Jesus Christ and the Mother of God; the gospel narrative of the Annunciation, which took place "to a virgin named Mary, betrothed to Joseph of the house of David" (Lk 1:27).

Why this deliberate exclusion, to use the gentlest word possible? A reasonable conjecture puts it down to false ecumenism. A disedifying story was told about ill-placed fun among some experts and observers on the subject of St. Joseph, joking especially about a fat book on him — it may have been Fr. Henry Filas' *The Man Closest To Jesus*, which is a work of scholarship.

So the Protestants would be appeased; or such was the hope. Not all of them were. The greatest Protestant theologian of our time, if not of all time, Karl Barth, was interviewed at the time on his views about St. Joseph. His reservations about Catholic devotion to Our Lady were well known, said the interviewer. So he felt as strongly on devotion to her spouse. Quite the contrary, replied

---

[4] How it was inserted is interesting. For generations requests had been sent to Rome to have the saint's name inserted in the Canon — and elsewhere also. When St. Pius X, whose baptismal name was Guiseppe, was asked, he refused, "no one has touched this Canon. Why did John XXIII decide *motu proprio* to add the name? On 10 November 1962, he was following the Council debates on closed circuit television. He saw Bishop Cule of Mostar, hesitant in speech, pleading for this inclusion of the saint's name in the Canon. Some bishops were tittering. But the Pope knew that this was a hero; he had been condemned by an unjust tribunal, was on a train deliberately wrecked to kill him and others, had his hips broken, he spent four years in prison. As from 8 December following, the name of St. Joseph appeared in the Roman Canon, now Eucharistic Prayer I.

the theologian. "I love St. Joseph. I hope that Pope John's decision to insert his name in the Canon of the Mass was covered by infallibility. When I meet Pope Paul VI, I intend to ask him to give prominence to the saint. Then he spoke an immortal word: "He protected the Child; he will protect the Church."[5]

A sharper criticism of the Council Fathers for their omission of St. Joseph in dealing with the Annunciation came from J.J. von Allmen of the University of Neuchatel in Switzerland, a Swiss Calvinist. To omit St. Joseph was to disregard the legal guarantor of the Davidic claim of Jesus the Messiah; he was not the physical, but certainly the legal, father of Jesus. Von Allmen also deplored the failure to put forward the saint as a model of holiness in the male sex, as Mary was so for women. We believe that she was a model for all.

In passing, be it noted that the Council behaved similarly to their teaching on Our Lady, again presumably for "ecumenical" reasons. Not only would the Fathers not accept the title Mediatress of all Graces, but on the last day of the debate, Cardinal Alfrink, supported by 150 others, asked that the word Mediatress be deleted — it had been put into the text along with other titles (Advocate, Helper, Benefactress) as a title under which she "is invoked in the Church."[6]

The Cardinal did not know that Our Lady has been styled Mediatress in the East since the fifth century, in the West since the eighth. He did not know that the greatest treatise on Mary's universal mediation was the work of a fourteenth century Orthodox theologian, Theophanes of Nicaea. The Council Fathers were gravely misled by a report from the drafting commission. They were told that the great Marian Pope, Pius XII, had never used the word Mediatress about Our Lady; he did so eight times. They were told that in the East the usage of the word was not supported by a theo-

---

[5] For Karl Barth cf. M. O'Carroll, *Theotokos*, p. 68ff.

[6] Cf. J.J. von Allmen, *Remarques sur la Constitution Dogmatique Lumen Gentium, Irenikon*, 39(1966) 22-23.

logical system. There is not a comparable system anywhere to that of Theophanes.[7]

<h2 style="text-align:center">(iii)</h2>

Was there similar disinformation in regard to the Sacred Heart of Jesus? The word disinformation, it is scarcely necessary to say, applies solely to preliminaries to formal conciliar action. There was no occasion for such an unhappy communication, for the subject that concerns us was at no time on the agenda, neither in pre-conciliar suggestions solicited from bishops and Catholic universities worldwide, nor, as has been stated, in textual drafting.

It is important for the life of the Church to pursue the inquiry: why the omission? The Sacred Heart of Jesus had united in Catholic life two powerful factors, papal teaching and the piety of the faithful. The piety of the faithful reflecting their belief is of immense significance; the word used by theologians is *sensus fidei*. The one who brought it into the front zone of Catholic thinking was the greatest intellectual convert to the Catholic Church in the nineteenth century, Cardinal Newman; one would not have sought sensitivity to common folk in the writings of such a one. But he saw the whole truth. In his paper, "On Consulting the Faithful in Matters of Doctrine," he explained that the belief held and professed by the laity, the body of church members, was vitally important.

Newman begins from the fact that the faithful are, on certain occasions, treated with "attention and consideration." He goes on: "Then follows the question, 'Why,' and the answer is *Viz.* because the body of the faithful is one of the witnesses of the tradition of revealed doctrine, and because their *consensus* through Christendom is the voice of the infallible Church." The tradition of the Apostles

---

[7] Cf. *Meditation, Mary Mediatress* in M. O'Carroll, *Theotokos*, 238ff. A stringent criticism of Vatican II, at the end of Session III, was made by a Greek theologian, Nikos Nissiotis, for their failure to produce a theology of the Holy Spirit; the author was editor of the *Ecumenical Review*, official organ of the World Council of Churches, 2(1965) *The main ecclesiological problems in the Second Vatican Council and the position of the non-Roman Churches facing it*, 31-62, esp. p. 48.

committed to the whole Church, manifests itself *per modum unius* in the various constituents and functions; "these include the people." Though none of these channels must be treated with disrespect, one must grant fully, Newman stated, "that the gift of discerning, discriminating, defining, promulgating, and enforcing any portion of that tradition resides solely in the *Ecclesia docens*."

Newman knew that Pius IX, before defining the dogma of the Immaculate Conception, had consulted the bishops of the whole Church: the Pope sought to be informed "concerning the devotion which animates your clergy and your people regarding the Immaculate Conception of the Blessed Virgin, and how ardently glows the desire that this doctrine be defined by the Apostolic See." Pius XII acted likewise before defining the dogma of the Assumption of Our Lady. John Paul II has encouraged the movement which seeks worldwide support for the final Marian dogma, Mary, Co-Redemptress Mediatress of all Graces, Advocate.

The Council Fathers of Vatican II were obliged by their own teaching to listen to the voice of the faithful, Newman had been misunderstood in Rome; he was vindicated by the Council: "The body of the faithful as a whole, anointed as they are by the Holy One (cf. Jn. 1,2:20,27) cannot err in matters of belief. Thanks to a supernatural sense of faith which characterizes the people as a whole, it manifests this unerring quality when from the bishops down to the last member of the laity, it shows universal agreement in matters of faith and morals. All this it does under the lead of a sacred teaching authority to which it loyally defers."[9]

(iv)

It may be argued that despite the massive witness of the faithful to the mystery of the Sacred Heart, the Council Fathers saw no need to reaffirm papal teaching. Two other considerations should have weighed with them. Their ecumenical interest must have informed them that the separated Churches of East and West do not have this devotion. Especially the Orthodox whose piety is expressed

---

[8]   ed. J. Coulson, London, 1961.
[9]   Constitution on the Church, 12.

in their icons, give clear evidence of a different, highly distinctive, very moving approach to the Saviour: he is the Pantocrator. The same false ecumenism which led to the exclusion of St. Joseph could and possibly did have a similar bad effect in regard to the Sacred Heart of Jesus. A better, a true, ecumenism would have dictated teaching to reassure Catholics and present their form of piety sympathetically to the others.

There is another reason why such teaching should have been issued. This was a great opportunity missed. The very intention to seek biblical warrant for everything should have prompted the Council Fathers to open an immense treasure of the Old Testament, the heart as the measure of the human being. We are now in a position to name the three great civilizations of the Ancient Mediterranean: that of law, Roman; that of the intellect, Greek; and the greatest, that of the heart, Jewish.

Is this wishful thinking? The sacred books of the Old Testament proclaim the resounding reply: the heart figures in eight hundred and fifty texts. One will prove instructive to the general reader. St. Thomas Aquinas taught that the Gospel of Jesus Christ is in its reward summarized in the fifth Beatitude, "Blessed are the pure in heart, they shall see God."[10] Jesus took this idea of "the pure in heart" from the Old Testament (cf. Ps 23(24):4; Ps 51:10).

Those who think that such a view minimizes Christ, questions his originality, should turn to a considerable volume of writing recently published. On what subject? The Jewishness of Jesus Christ. With some hyperbole one may say that it has taken two thousand years to discover the most obvious thing about him: He was a Jew; God became a Jew! He was therefore not only the fulfillment of the messianic hope of Israel, but he was steeped in the verbal expression of the truth which he, the Word of God, with the Father and the Holy Spirit, had given to his creatures.[11] We shall attempt to explore the incalculable riches of the Old Testament teaching on the heart, as the revelation of the human being. This is a task which calls for much cooperation. Just now it

---

[10] *Summa contra Gentes*, Bk III, ch. 25.

[11] Cf. M. O'Carroll, *Verbum Caro*, Liturgical Press, 1992, 82-86, *The Jewishness of Jesus*.

is important to realize, as fully as possible, that through the centuries, as Jesus reveals to us, his followers, the mystery of his heart, he still speaks as a Jew, the ultimate perfection of humanity in Jewry. We must bear in mind when he opens his heart to St. Gertrude or St. Margaret Mary Alacoque, that there is no rupture whatever between his thinking as a Jew of the final generation of hope, hope fulfilled in him, and his illumination of those who would come to have faith in him and live in him through the Christian centuries. It may be too much to hope that we shall achieve full understanding of his revelation of the heart; this may be postponed until all Israel comes to him. Recognition of our difficulty need not impede our effort.

As has already been mentioned, it is to the Popes that we owe such initiatives. One cannot think of Vatican II proclaiming St. Joseph patron of the universal Church, or of workers: it must be admitted

(v)

Meanwhile we have another avenue towards the truth. In John Paul II, teacher on the Sacred Heart of Jesus, we have an acknowledged expert in a branch of philosophy which is highly instructive, phenomenology. This is not praise of a Pope by a Catholic because he is a Pope. An important French encyclopedia on philosophers has a substantial entry on the Pope, noting that he is the author of fifty special studies on the subject; he published an academic work on Max Scheler, a phenomenologist, whose theory he compared with that of St. Thomas Aquinas. His work, before his election as Pope, "The Acting Person," appeared in the *Analecta Husserliana,* and was written as a contribution to phenomenological anthropology.

Where phenomenology joins the anthropology of the Old Testament, as this was received and ennobled by the Messiah, is in the concept of the human being judged by his or her interaction in life with others. The heart was the word which denoted this profound reality, a reality beyond the Roman legal system, or the magnificent, but inevitably abstract, even static, Greek dissection of the human composite. What is more important is that the heart was the opening of the human being to the very source of life, Almighty God. This is clearly expressed by St. Luke as he concludes his narrative of two vital moments in the life of Our Lady, the first recognition of Jesus as Saviour by her people; and his decision to continue in subjection to her and Joseph: "But Mary kept in mind all these things pondering them in her heart" (2:19); "And his mother

9

kept all these things carefully in her heart" (2:51). Her heart as that of a true Jewess, responded at once to a divine intervention. Rightly did the Fathers of the Church maintain that with her heart she have her Fiat in the moment of the Annunciation. For we must recognise that the Jewishness of Mary as well as that of Jesus.

We are considering perspectives which should have influenced the Fathers of Vatican II to publish a teaching on the Sacred Heart of Jesus. Further analysis leads to an enlightening contrast; here too the parallel with St. Joseph helps. Not only did the Council not make any doctrinal mention of him; it would not be in the tenor of their documents to issue detailed pastoral or devotional directives. As has already been mentioned, it is to the Popes that we owe such initiatives. One cannot think of Vatican II proclaiming St. Joseph patron of the universal Church, or of workers; it must be admitted that the action of Pius IX was a response to petitions "renewed during the sacred Ecumenical Council of the Vatican (i.e. Vatican I) by all groups of the faithful, and - what is more important — by many of our Venerable Brethren, the Cardinals and Bishops of the Holy Roman Church.[12]

Is there contradiction between papal and conciliar attitudes and texts? I see them, in the best moments, as complementary. I would have expected teaching on St. Joseph from Vatican II, in conciliar terms, expressing essential truths in the theological idiom of such an assembly. We got nothing.

As in studying the history of past Councils of the Church, we have to consider all the elements of a given situation, within which such teaching emerged, so now we have to consider all that surrounded the sessions of Vatican II. The Council was heavily influenced by the *periti* (theological experts), and these may not always have been sympathetic to a purely pastoral idea like the Sacred Heart of Jesus — which is not to deny the valuable work of the *periti* in so many sectors.

But the Council was representative of the Catholic Church in this century and it emphasized the importance of the Church as the

---

[12] Dordrecht, London, Boston, 1979, collection named for Edmund Husserl, founder of Phenomenology.

People of God. The People of God, through their prayers, through their favoured iconography, through their instinctive attitude to the Saviour, and their spontaneous spiritual image of him, were totally centred on the Sacred Heart.

If we did not expect from the Council a teaching on the Sacred Heart of Jesus in language identical with the great papal documents which have treated of this mystery, *Annum Sacrum* of Leo XII, *Miserentissimus Deus* of Pius XI, *Haurietis Aquas* of Pius XII, we had a right to hear the voice of this great assembly representing the Church which claims our total allegiance, proclaiming to the whole world the central dynamic force which gives it life, power, endurance, attractiveness. As with St. Joseph, we got nothing. A Council speaking to the world of today refused even to mention the very source of its existence. For the Church of which it was a spokesman, would not exist as it did if it had not been consecrated to the Sacred Heart of Jesus; devotion, in the true, profound meaning of the term, to the Sacred Heart of Jesus, enlivened the very best elements in its fabric, was the guarantor of its credibility to those searching for God, but a God sensitive to every distressing element of the human condition, a God of compassion.

(vi)

There was then a void in the aftermath of the Council. In a void strange things can happen. Those who had no strong belief or enthusiasm in regard to this mystery grew more apathetic, if not totally indifferent. Some bent on ecumenism at any cost may have thought that it would be better to marginalise a practice and spirituality not found explicitly in the other Christian churches or communions. There may have been a small number of iconoclasts, who stop at nothing.

The loss was incalculable. A mighty source of inspiration, and of defense in face of the spreading apostasy of our time was neglected, in places despised. A generation arose with no instruction on the Sacred Heart of Jesus, no awareness of the army of heroes and heroines with which this unique Benefactor had blessed our Church, no idea of how the quality of Catholic life had been moulded on this model.

Is there a way back? There has to be for those who hope for a renewal of the Church, a renewal to be effected in Christian unity, drawing on the tested entirely valid traditions of each Church and communion.

(vii)

Let us then recall certain salient points in the growth of the Catholic tradition on this particular all-embracing ideal. We begin with St. Gertrude the Great (d. 1302), one of the great mystics in the history of the Church, worthy representative of the thirteenth, greatest century in the spiritual life of Europe. Before her, there had been many intimations by great saints like St. Bernard and St. Bonaventure of the mystery enclosed in the Heart of Jesus; it was generally in contemplation of the pierced side of the Saviour in his Passion.

Among the many revelations received by St. Gertrude, one has been singled out as particularly significant. It was in the course of a vision, on the feast of St. John the Evangelist, when this saint appeared to her and led her to the Saviour. Together they were in the presence of his Heart, conscious of his heart-beats. St. John said to her, "Behold the holy of holies who draws to himself all that is good in heaven and on earth." St. Gertrude asked him if he had experienced the attractiveness of the divine Heart. Informed that he had, she asked, "Wherefore, then, have you kept such absolute silence about this, that you have never written anything, however little it might be, that would make it understood, at least for the profit of our souls?" St. John replied: "My mission was to deliver to the Church, in her first age, a simple word on the uncreated Word of God the Father, that would suffice until the end of the world to satisfy the understanding of the whole human race, yet without any person ever succeeding in fully understanding it. But to tell of the sweetness of these heartbeats has been reserved for the present time, so that in hearing of these things the world that is growing old and whose love is weakening may be revived."[13]

---

[13] Apud Jean Bainvel, *Devotion to the Sacred Heart of Jesus*, London, 1924, p. 140.

St. Gertrude did not have a mission to the universal Church, such as would be given later to St. Margaret Mary. But through her writings she serves as God's instrument to stir our wonder, our love, before this sublime mystery of immeasurable divine generosity and compassion. Thus as editor described her experience:

"Sometimes the divine Heart appeared to her as a treasury which contained all riches; sometimes as a lyre touched by the Holy Spirit, at the sound of which the most Holy Trinity and the whole court of heaven rejoiced. Again it is as a flowing spring whose waters bear refreshment to the souls in purgatory, strengthening graces to the souls who are fighting on earth, and those torrents of delight with which the elect of the heavenly Jerusalem are inebriated. It is as a golden censer whence arise as many different odours of incense as there are races of people for whom our Saviour has suffered the death of the Cross. Another time it is an altar on which the faithful lay their offerings, the elect their homage, the angels their reverential awe, and upon which the eternal High Priest immolates himself; it is a lamp suspended between heaven and earth; it is a chalice from which the saints drink, but not the angels, who nevertheless receive delight from it. In this divine Heart was conceived and elaborated the *Pater Noster*, the Lord's prayer. It supplies for all the homage that we have neglected to offer to God, to the Blessed Virgin, to the saints. To discharge all our obligations, this Sacred Heart becomes our servant, our guarantee; in it alone our works acquire that perfection, that dignity, which renders them pleasing to the divine majesty; through it alone flow all the graces that can descend on earth. Finally, it is the pleasant abode, the sacred sanctuary that is opened to souls when they leave this world, that in it they may be preserved for all eternity in ineffable delights."[14]

(viii)

We shall turn now to the saint most widely known as the apostle of the Heart of Jesus, St. Margaret Mary Alacoque. But let us note that she did not work in a total void. A historian puts it thus: "St.

[14] *Ibid.* p. 138.

Margaret Mary did not invent devotion to the Sacred Heart; it already existed. Before his revelation to her, our Lord had already revealed his Heart to some chosen souls, and had shown them the riches contained in it, Christians, while meditating on the mysterious wound in the side, had seen therein the wounded Heart; had understood that it afforded a refuge to guilty or weary souls, and the treasures that it contained; had perceived in the bodily wound the wound inflicted by love; lastly, had come to the knowledge and the sight of the divine Heart — most lovable and loving, the expressive symbol, the epitome of the virtues and the life of Christ."

In this period between St. Gertrude and the saint of Paray-le-Monial, special attention must be given to St. Jean Eudes, who "had taught the people devotion to the Sacred Heart, at first by means of devotion to the Heart of Mary, showing them in her Heart the divine Heart of her Son, and then, by means of a special feast in honour of that adorable Heart, so that in this as in other things, they were led quite naturally to Jesus through Mary."

St. Margaret Mary's mission to the Church was supported by Blessed Claude de la Colombiere, a Jesuit. She received many apparitions, two noteworthy. The first great apparition took place on the feast of St. John the Evangelist, probably in 1673; she was in Paray-le-Monial, a convent of the Visitation since 1671.

The saint wrote of being allowed "to rest on his Heart with his beloved disciple, and [of Jesus] giving her his Heart, his cross, and his love." The Sacred Heart then made one of the self-revelations of all history: "My divine Heart is so inflamed with love for men, and for you in particular, that not being able any longer to restrain within itself the flames of its ardent charity, it must spread them everywhere through your means, and manifest itself to men that they may be enriched with its precious treasures." It is all that is necessary "to rescue them from the abyss of perdition." He added: "I have chosen you as an abyss of unworthiness and of ignorance for the accomplishment of this great design, that thus all may be done by me."

In a second great apparition the saint learned of "the ardent desire which [the Sacred Heart] had of being loved by men, and of rescuing them from the path of perdition along which Satan drives them in crowds;" this had "made him form this design of manifesting his Heart to men with all the treasures of love, of mercy, of grace, of sanctification, and of salvation that it contains." Jesus asked that he be honoured" under the figure of this heart of flesh." Graces and blessings would be given to those who honour the image of his Sacred Heart.

In the third great apparition the saint heard the call for reparation; then too Jesus asked for the reception of Holy Communion on the First Friday of the month, a practice which would be linked with devotion to his Sacred Heart. The Lord expressed to the saint his desire that she should share in the mortal sadness that he felt in the Garden of Olives. "To accompany me in that humble prayer which I offered to my Father at that time in the midst of all my anguish, you will rise between eleven o'clock and midnight, and you will prostrate yourself with me, your face to the ground, for an hour, both to appease the divine anger by asking mercy for sinners, and to soften in some way the bitter sorrow that I felt at being abandoned by my Apostles . . . And during this hour you will do what I shall point out to you."

The requests were made personally to the saint, but they will, in due course, be given universal import.

Finally, we have to consider what is called *The Great Apparition*. On this occasion, the saint was before the Blessed Sacrament. She experienced an outpouring by the Lord on her of his "favours exceeding all measure. It was during this apparition that the saint heard these words which are often quoted: "Behold this Heart which has so loved men, which has spared nothing, even to being exhausted and consumed, in order to testify to them its love. And the great number of them make no other return than ingratitude, by their coldness and their forgetfulness of me in this Sacrament of love. But what is still more painful to me is that it is hearts who are consecrated to me who use me thus."

Then came the request which would make liturgical history: "It is because of this that I ask you to have the first Friday after the Octave of Corpus Christi kept as a special feast in honour of my Heart, by receiving Communion on that day and making it a reparation of honour for all the insults offered to my Heart during the time that it has been exposed on altars."[15]

---

[15] J. Bainvel, *op. cit.*, pp. 17-22.

Chapter II
Interpretation

(i)

Pius XI once said that devotion to the Sacred Heart is the synthesis of the whole Christian religion.[1] Is this how we shall interpret the elements which have been selected to give an idea of the rich, varied background to a unique subject? We are not dealing with one of the many forms of piety which have been proposed to Catholics, a matter of free choice to them. To appreciate its uniqueness, which is not to claim complete understanding, we have the help of two teachers who approach the subject in perspectives varying with the philosophical outlook, Pius XII and John Paul II.

Pius XII's Encyclical, as has been said already, was a landmark; in contents it is magisterial. The Pope centres his theology of the Sacred Heart on love. He sees this love already manifest in the Old Testament: "However, this love of God, forgiving, patient, wondrously tender, which, though roused to anger by the people of Israel heaping sin upon sin, nevertheless never casts them off altogether, does indeed seem passionate and carried away; and yet, it was but a harbinger of that burning charity which the Redeemer, promised to men, was to pour out upon all from his love-filled Heart, and which was to be both the foundation of the New Covenant and the pattern of our love for him. For indeed only he who is the Only-begotten of the Father and the Word made flesh 'full of grace and truth' (Jn 1:14) could come to men groaning under the weight of numberless sins and miseries, and could from his human

---

[1] Pius XII wrote in the Encyclical *Haurietis Aquas*: "With this primary truth (the Hypostatic Union) truly established, we see that the Heart of Jesus is the Heart of a divine Person, namely the Word Incarnate. It therefore represents and places before our gaze all the love in which he has enfolded us, and in which he still enfolds us today. For this reason, devotion to the Sacred Heart must be considered the perfect practical expression of the Christian religion."

nature, united hypostatically to a divine Person, open to human-kind a 'fountain of living water' copiously to irrigate the barren earth and to turn it into a flowering and fruitful paradise."[2]

Pursuing his theme through Sacred Scripture and the Fathers of the Church, the Pope sets forth his thought thus:

"Therefore the Heart of the Word made flesh is rightly looked upon as the principal token and sign of that threefold love where-with the divine Redeemer ceaselessly loves both his Eternal Father and all mankind. It is the sign of that divine love which he shares with the Father and with the Holy Spirit, but which in him only, that is in the Word which was made flesh, is made manifest to us in a frail and corruptible human body, since 'in him dwelleth all the fullness of the Godhead corporeally' (Col 2:9). It is moreover the sign of that white-hot charity which was infused into Christ's hu-man soul, and which enriches his human will. The acts of this charity are illumined and guided by Christ's twofold most perfect knowl-edge, and that is to say his beatific knowledge and his bestowed or infused knowledge. And finally his Heart is a sign — and this in a more direct and natural way — of his emotional affection, since the body of Jesus Christ, formed by the work of the Holy Spirit in the womb of the Virgin Mary, enjoyed in the fullest degree the power of feeling and perceiving more perfectly in fact than the bodies of all other men."[3]

This is the eminently satisfying authoritative counterpart to the words recorded by St. Margaret Mary, "Behold this Heart which has so loved men..." We shall gain by following the further exposi-tion of the theme by the Pope. Hear him on the Church: "The Sa-cred Heart of Jesus, then, partakes most intimately in the life of the Word made flesh, and therefore, no less than the other members of his nature, is as it were, an instrument which the Godhead has taken up and uses in the work of his grace and his omnipotence. There can therefore be no doubt that this Heart of Jesus is the lawful sym-bol of that boundless charity which moved our Saviour to shed his blood and so to enter into mystical marriage with the Church ... And so from the wounded Heart of the Redeemer was born the

---

[2] *Op. cit.*
[3] *Op. cit.*

Church, as the dispenser of the Blood of our Redemption; and from the same Heart flows in copious abundance the grace of the Sacraments, from which the Church's children drink supernatural life, as we say in the sacred Liturgy: 'From risen Heart is born the Church, espoused to Christ.' And 'Who from out his Heart pours grace.'"

Quoting St. Thomas Aquinas on the wounded side of Christ, from which flowed water for washing and blood for redeeming, the Pope comments: "Now what is written here of the side of Christ, wounded and laid open by the soldier, is also applicable to his Heart, which the lance's thrust certainly reached, in as much as the soldier's purpose in wielding it was to make certain beyond all doubt that Jesus Christ crucified was dead. Hence the wound in the Sacred Heart of the dead Christ is for all times a vivid image of that spontaneous charity whereby God gave his only-begotten Son to redeem men, and whereby Christ has loved us so vehemently that he immolated himself for us a bleeding victim on Calvary's hill. 'Christ hath loved us and hath delivered himself for us, an oblation and a sacrifice to God for an odour of sweetness.'" (Eph 5:2)[4]

The Pope draws our attention to the Heart of Christ in glory: "Our Saviour has now ascended into heaven, his body bedecked with the splendours of eternal glory; he has taken his throne at the Father's right hand. But he has not ceased to love his spouse, the Church, with that furnace of love wherewith his Heart still throbs. On his hands, on his feet and in his side he bears the glorious marks of his wounds, showing forth his threefold victory over Satan, sin and death. And in the precious repository of his Heart are stored the fruits of that threefold triumph, even the boundless merits which he poured out in flowing abundance on redeemed mankind."[5]

(ii)

It is not often recalled that Pius XII gave a deep Trinitarian insight in his teaching on the Sacred Heart, unique thus far in the literature; it was not appreciated because the Catholic Church officially and throughout the body of the faithful was neglectful of the

---

[4] *Op. cit.*

[5] *Op. cit.*

Holy Spirit: we are not far from the days when a French spiritual writer, Mgr. Landrieux published a book entitled *Le divin meconnu* (in English, *The Forgotten Paraclete*), when a Pope, Pius XI, could issue an Encyclical on Christian Unity without once mentioning the Holy Spirit; contrast, be it said in passing, John Paul II's Encyclical on the same subject, *Ut Unum Sint*, wherein the Holy Spirit is spoken of forty times.

Here then are the words of Pius XII: "After his triumphal ascent to the right hand of his Father, the gift of the Holy Spirit, sent upon his disciples, is the first outstanding sign of his munificent charity. For, after ten days, the Spirit, even the Paraclete given by the heavenly Father, came down upon them, where they were gathered in the Cenacle, according to his promise at the Last Supper: 'I will ask the Father, and he shall give you another Paraclete, that he may abide with you forever' (Jn 14:16). And this Paraclete Spirit, since he is the mutual personal Love, that is of the Father for the Son and of the Son for the Father, is sent by both Father and Son; and clothing himself, as it were, in the appearances of tongues of fire, he pours into their hearts an abundance of divine charity and of other heavenly gifts. The torrent of this divine charity rises also in the Heart of our Saviour, 'in whom are hidden all the treasures of wisdom and knowledge' (Col 2:3). For this charity is the gift both of the Heart of Jesus and of his Spirit, who is indeed the Spirit of the Father and of the Son. From this Spirit comes the origin of the Church and its marvelous spreading before the face of all those nations and peoples who were sunk in the degradation of idolatry, fraternal hatred, violence and moral corruption. This divine charity is the inestimable gift of the Heart of Christ and of his Spirit."

This is the first time in a document from the Teaching authority that the Sacred Heart of Jesus is so closely linked with the Holy Spirit. The Pope then mentions some of the beneficiaries of this "divine charity."

"To the Apostles and Martyrs it imparted a fortitude strengthened by which they strove even unto death, heroically endured, to preach the truth of the gospel and seal it with their blood. In the Doctors of the Church it instilled a burning zeal to defend and shed light upon Catholic truth. It has nourished the virtues of Confessors and roused them to wonderful works, most profitable to their own and others' eternal and temporal happiness. And lastly, it has persuaded the Virgins freely and with joyful hearts to leave behind them the pleasure of the body, in order to consecrate themselves entirely to the love of their heavenly Bridegroom. This divine charity flows from the Heart of the Word made flesh, and is poured out by the Holy Spirit in the hearts of all believers."

"The Heart," the Pope continues, "still lives and beats and is indissolubly united to the Person of the Divine Word, and in him and through him with his divine will. Wherefore, since the Heart of Christ overflows with divine and human love, and is surpassing rich in all the treasures of grace which our Redeemer acquired by his life, his sufferings and his death, it is therefore the perennial fount of that charity which his Spirit pours out upon all the members of his Mystical Body."[6]

(iii)

John Paul's teaching is complementary to that of Pius XII: "Through the work of the Holy Spirit, the humanity of Christ, Son of the eternal Father, took shape in the womb of the Virgin of Nazareth. Through the work of the Holy Spirit, the Heart took shape in this humanity; the Heart, which is the central organ of the human organism of Christ, and at the same time the true symbol of his interior life: his thoughts, his will, his sentiments. Through this Heart the humanity of Christ is, in a particular way, the temple of God, and, at the same time, through this Heart it remains open to men and to all that is human."

Elsewhere, Pope John Paul gives us an idea of how the heart may be understood in the terms of the philosophy of which he is an expert. Thought structures serving divine revelation must have the flexibility which derives from mystery. There must be recognition for the wholeness and milt-dimensional reality of the Heart. Thus speaks John Paul II: "The mystery of the Cross on Golgotha and the mystery of the Cross in the Heart of the Mother of the Crucified One cannot be read in any other way: only in the perspective of eternal Wisdom is this mystery clarified for our faith. Indeed it

---

[6] *Op. cit.*

becomes the beam of a special light in human history, in the midst of a people's destiny on earth. This light is, first of all, in the Heart of Christ lifted on the Cross. This light, reflected by the power of a special love, shines forth in the Heart of the Sorrowful Mother at the foot of the Cross."

The Pope was speaking to Canadian Catholics (September 15, 1984, Toronto). Later, he dealt with another aspect of the same theme: "This cry of the Son's Heart and of his Mother's Heart — a cry which from the human standpoint would reject the Cross — is expressed in the Psalm of today's liturgy. This Psalm is a cry for salvation, for help, for deliverance from the snare of evil (Ps 31:3,4,16). Since the words of the Psalm reflect 'human' truth of the Hearts of the Son and of the Mother, they also express an act of absolute entrusting of God — dedication to God. This dedication is even stronger than the cry for deliverance (Ps 31:15). This awareness — 'you are my God. Into your hands I commend my spirit,' prevails absolutely in the Heart of the Son 'lifted up' on the Cross, and in the Mother's Heart humanly emptied by the Son's crucifixion."[7]

(iv)

We have to explore the Old Testament record of the civilization of the Heart. We have seen that a key precept of the Lord, "Blessed are the pure of heart," was taken from the Psalms. As the individual attempts to relate to God, he does so through his heart: "I delight to do thy will, O my God, thy law is within my heart" (Ps 40:8). The response of the Lord is in equivalent terms: "But this is the covenant which I will make with the house of Israel after those days, says the Lord: I will put my law within them and I will write it upon their hearts, and I will be their God and they will be my people" (Jer 31:33). "A new heart I will give you and a new spirit I will put within you; I will take out of your flesh the heart of stone, and I will give you a heart of flesh" (Ex 36:26).

John L. McKenzie, a great biblical scholar, gives some examples of how manifold human experience is in this world seen through the heart: "The heart is glad or cheerful (Jgs 18:20; Pr

---

[7] Cf. *Verbum Caro*, M. O'Carroll, article *The Sacred Heart*, pp. 158-161.

15:13); it experiences religious exultation (1 S 2:1; Pss 13:6; 28:7; 84:3). The heart is made merry by wine (Rt 3:7; Ps 104:15). The heart feels grief and sadness (1 S 1:8; Ps 13:3; Pr 14:10,13,15; 15:13; Je 8:18), disappointment (Pr 13:12), impatience and vexation (Ps 73:21), worry and anguish (Pss 25:17; 55:5; Je 4:19; 23:9), anger (Dt 19:6; 2 K 6:11), hatred (Lv 19:17), fear (Dt 28:67; Ps 27:3; I S 4:13). A firm or strong heart is a sign of courage (Pss 27:14; 31:25; Am 2:16)....The heart is the source of thoughts, desires, and deeds (Dt 15:9). One's plan or purpose lies in the heart (Is 10:7)....Wisdom, discernment, and knowledge are seated in the heart (Ez 28:3; Dt 8:5; 1 K 3:12)....Moral qualities are attributed to the heart as the seat of decision. It may be pure (Pss 24:4; 73:1), 'whole,' that is, sincere (Gn 20:5) or upright (Dt 9:5; 1 K 3:6). Thus, a man is what his heart is....Yahweh examines the heart (Ps 17:3; Je 12:3); indeed, only Yahweh can know the heart, which is deceitful above all things (Je 17:9f)."[8]

(v)

What of the New Testament witness? Fr. I. de la Potterie comments thus: "Like other recent theologians, Von Balthasar seems to assume that Jn 19:31-37 is the most important biblical passage on which devotion to the Sacred Heart is based. These authors give us theological examinations of the importance of the heart in biblical anthropology or of the symbolism of blood and water. It must be noted, however, that the word 'heart' is not even mentioned in this text. To be sure, the open side of Jesus, or the blood and water which flow from it, are extremely rich symbols; but even so, they are no more than symbols or signs. Moreover, they are associated with the moment immediately following Jesus' death on the cross. We are told nothing of the living Heart of the earthly Jesus, of the interior life of Jesus the man, in the course of his public life. This is where new developments in Christology can make their precious contribution."

Fr. de la Potterie proposed that the subject be approached from two viewpoints arising from contemporary Christology: the attempt to base Christology on the historical Jesus, recovering the entire

---

[8] *Dictionary of the Bible*, London, New York, 1965, p. 343f.

dimension of his actual life — while avoiding the snares of historicism, and the attempt of scholars to interpret Chalcedon, without rejecting its essential meaning.

As the biblical scholar says, the first approach brings us straight into the question of the consciousness of Jesus. "To talk about a person's deep consciousness amounts to the same as speaking of what he has in his heart, and this also holds true for the Heart of Jesus. This reminds us that we are dealing with Jesus' consciousness and hence also invites us to be less exclusively concerned with the anatomical reality of his physical Heart, about which it would be remembered that the New Testament says nothing; whereas, as we shall see, it provides quite a number of pointers which make it possible for us to glimpse at Jesus' interior life."[9]

On 8 December, 1985, the International Theological Commission issued an important document on the subject of Jesus' Consciousness, some extracts from which will help to illustrate Fr. de la Potterie's thesis: "The life of Jesus witnesses to consciousness of his filial relationship with the Father. His behaviour and his words which are those of the perfect 'servant' imply an authority which far surpasses that of the ancient prophets and reverts to God alone. Jesus derived this incomparable excellence from his singular relationship with God, whom he calls 'my Father.' He was conscious of being the only Son of God, and in this sense, of being himself God."

"The consciousness which Jesus has of himself coincides with the consciousness of his mission. This has much deeper significance than consciousness of a prophetic mission received at a particular moment, even were it from the 'womb of his mother' (Jeremiah, cf. Jer 1:5 the Baptist cf Lk 1:15; Paul cf. Gal 1:15).

"The consciousness which Jesus has of his mission implies then the consciousness of his 'pre-existence.' In fact, the mission is its 'prolongation.' The human consciousness of his mission 'translates, so to speak, the eternal relationship with the Father into the language of a human life.

"The relationship of the Word incarnate with the Father assumes in the first place the mediation of the Holy Spirit. The Spirit

---

[9] In *Towards a Civilization of Love: Proceedings of the International Congress on the Heart of Jesus*, Toulouse, July 24-28, 1981, English tr., San Francisco, Milwaukee, 1985, p.48.

must then be in the consciousness of Jesus insofar as he is Son. His very human existence already is the result of an action by the Spirit; since the Baptism of Jesus, all his work — whether action or passion among men, or communion of prayer with the Father — is accomplished only in and through the Spirit (Lk 4:18; Acts 10:38; cf. Mk 1:12; Mt 12:28). The Son knows that in the accomplishment of the good will of the Father, the Spirit guides and upholds him to the Cross. There, with his earthly mission achieved, he handed over (*paredoken*) his 'spirit' (*pneuma*)(Jn 19:30) in which some people read an insinuation of the gift of the Spirit. After his resurrection and ascension, he becomes a man, glorified which as God he was from all eternity, a 'vivifying' Spirit (1 Cor 14:45; 2 Cor 3:17), Lord empowered to distribute, in sovereign manner, the Spirit to raise us to the dignity of sons in himself."[10]

This teaching showing the mysterious wealth of human experience within the soul of Jesus, true God and true man, answers the biblical scholar's first question. As to his suggestion about reflection on the dogma of Chalcedon, that Jesus Christ was a divine Person in two natures, human and divine, he has this quotation from another author to offer: "This historical interpretation of Christology presupposes the ontological one, for the history of Jesus would lose all its theological meaning if it were not the human history of a divine Person. Our texts show that the Chalcedonian dogma is in no way called into question again, but is, on the contrary, perfectly incorporated into the proposed interpretation. The Word's human freedom considered within actual history belongs in point of fact to the nature taken on by him, and is even its innermost centre. This is truly the 'heart' of Christ's holy humanity. It is possible to build an authentic spirituality of the 'Sacred Heart" on a dogmatic foundation as solid as this.[11]

---

[10] Full text in M. O'Carroll, *Verbum Caro*, 38-43, excerpt, p. 40.

[11] *Op. cit.*, p. 50; on the important subject of the civilization of the heart cf. W.E. Lynch, *Catholic Encyclopedia*, VI, p. 965; J.H. Bauer, *Encyclopedia of Biblical Theology*, I 360f, article by J.H. Bauer; F.H. van Heyenfieldt, *Het Hart in het Oud Testament*, Leiden 1950; J.P.E. Petersen, *Israel, Its Life and Culture*, New York, 1959, I, pp. 99-181; E. Trestomant, *A Study of Hebrew Thought*, tr. M.F. Gibson, New York, 1960, pp. 83-124.

(vi)

With the guidance of the Popes and the insights of Scripture scholars, we are encouraged to continue reflection on the awe-inspiring yet deeply touching mystery. We need not set out an extensive phenomenological analysis; we may borrow a little from the method. It will help the attainment of a conscious, permanent realization of the Savior's divine Heart central to our life. It is valuable to grasp how a single concept and word may express the impact of a human person on others, how it may clarify the focus of attraction, when this is strongest. Seen thus the heart is the very centre of the individual's being, the sanctuary of self-awareness in which is summarized and condensed the concrete essence of man the vital thrust into the existence of others.

The heart gives some understanding of those whose whole being is caught in a testing ordeal or crisis; some fail because they lose heart, others are lion-hearted and survive. We are in the presence of the mystery enshrined in each member of the human race, where there is self-awareness but not total self-knowledge, as phrases like "I do not know how I did it" manifest. When we come to consider the one human being who was also God, the mystery is, to us, manifold; to him all is Light, for he is the Light of the world (Jn. 9:5).

His physical Heart, as his whole corporeal being, had not the slightest flaw or weakness, was entirely true in function and response to his soul. His psychic and physical structure had a unity to which only one other person had a resemblance, the one whose Immaculate Heart was modeled on his Sacred Heart.

We can then approach his Heart in many ways; we have here a world of sheer transcendence, which we shall enter fully only in the final glory, to know the existence of which and to aspire to some knowledge matching our frailty, is divine condescension.

Christ was a man of great heart, the "Lion of the Fold of Judah." He radiated power and he was a miracle worker, the supreme exorcist. From him, about him, there was an aura of tenderness which drew the downcast, broken, sinful to him as his magnetism cast a spell on children.

Yet within this assemblage of qualities which so admirably fitted him for a social role, there was the majesty of the Godhead;

the Godhead endowed him with three fundamental attributes, in each of which his Heart is our hope: he the great High Priest, the Universal sovereign King, the supreme Prophet of divine truth, as Vatican II has put it, the "Mediator and the fullness of all revelation."

We have but begun to penetrate the mysterious depths of this threefold endowment; the collective genius of all humanity given millennia will not exhaust this sublime reality. It is the task of his accredited teachers, and it is the task of each individual soul, to seek some entry to the privileged sanctuary of his priestly, regal and luminous Heart. How readily we can believe that from this Heart will yet come untold, wholly unforeseen, benefits.

We cannot know who will come among us to manifest in startling manner the inexhaustible efficacy and fecundity of the sacerdotal Heart of Christ; nor can we anticipate the moments chosen by the Father to demonstrate to the world the meaning of authority, royal authority seen and lived as service through the Heart of Christ. Finally, who would dare try even to outline the treasures of knowledge which Christ, the glorious Prophet will draw for us from his adorable Heart.

Chapter III
The Eucharist

The instinct of the faithful, and the special experience of privileged disciples direct our attention to the Eucharistic Heart of Jesus. Let us first recall the immense mystery enshrined in this word "Eucharist." Celebrated on our altars and on those of our Orthodox brethren, this is the perfect sacrifice. The human person is by the innermost structure of his or her being oriented towards such a public religious act. This explains the vast, varied array of sacrificial rites which history and comparative religion make known; it also explains the important place which sacrificial rituals had in the ages of the ancient covenant.

What constitutes sacrifice? Theorists of the subject have singled out these elements: the gift of the human being to the deity; communion with the deity in the sacrificial banquet; life released from the victim, transmitted to the deity and conferred upon the worshippers. An official, a priest, performs the rite for the people.

We need not delay on the discussions of theologians on these different elements. It suffices to say that sacrifice responds to a universal human yearning, human before a corruption which may set in after the full truth has been known and rejected.

In the Eucharist the followers of Christ have the perfect sacrifice, priest and victim identified in God made man, each celebration reenacting the central moment of the history of humankind: Calvary with the Resurrection making one entity, the Paschal Mystery. Through all that led up to this the Heart of Jesus, in its plenary meaning, was central. When the sacrifice is continued on our altars, this central role is fulfilled before the eyes of faith. Every Catholic assisting at Mass, participating as correct present-day liturgy facilitates, is one with the Sacred Heart of Jesus in the act by which he changed the entire history of the world; he reversed the tide of decadence flowing from Adam and Eve, instituted a new order in which human beings would achieve their initial divinely ordained destiny, become images of the living God.

The Eucharist is also a Sacrament. It is the most perfect of the Sacraments, for three reasons: whereas all the Sacraments give grace to the soul, it gives not only grace, but the Author of grace; all the others are, in one way or another, directed towards it; uniquely it carries a promise of salvation, "If anyone eats of this bread he shall live forever, and the bread that I will give is my flesh for the life of the world" (Jn. 6:52).

The believing Christian who receives Jesus Christ in Holy Communion is then closest to the Heart of Jesus. When he or she is present at the Blessed Sacrament publicly exposed he or she worships the Heart of Jesus giving himself totally to those who love him, yearn for him as their Redeemer, desire that he be given the honour due to the Lord of all creation, the King of angels and of men. In their cult of the Sacred Heart Christians honour, serve, and love this Heart as the immediate source and inspiration of his entire redemptive and sanctifying mission and achievement. In their devotion to the Eucharistic Heart they look to the sublime gift wherein all that is embodied, himself in the Eucharist, not only his gift, but his real presence, his sacrificial immolation, his union with us in our sacramental communion.

(ii)

Some history is, on the subject, illuminating. Already in the seventeenth century, St. John Eudes (d. 1680) spoke of the Heart of Jesus as a furnace of love for us in the most holy Sacrament. In that age too, according to present knowledge, *Cor eucharisticum* and *Cor Jesu eucharistici* were used for the first time. They are found in the work of a German parish priest, Anthony Gunther (1655-c.1740).[1]

---

[1] In his work, *Speculum amoris et doloris in sacratissimo ac divinissimo Corde Jesu incarnati, eucharistici et crucifixi orbi Chrisitano propositum*, Augsburg, 1706, ed. 4, 1743; about the same time, a French Maurist, Jean-Paul du Sault (1650-1724) wrote of the "divine Heart of Jesus in the Most Holy Sacrament of the Altar" in his *Entretiens avec Jesus Christ dans le Tres-Saint Sacrament de l'autel*, Toulouse, 5 vol., 1701-1703.

The private revelation of a devout French lady, Sophie Prouvier, had an effect in spreading devotion to the Eucharistic Heart; a prayer composed by her in 1854 was in that year indulgenced by Mgr. Mabile, Bishop of Saint-Claude. Sermons, one of the first by St. Pierre-Julien Eymard, Founder of the Blessed Sacrament Fathers, articles, papers at national and international Eucharistic Congresses, took up the idea and expounded or defended it. Official action was not lacking. Pius IX in 1868 indulgenced an invocation to the Eucharistic Heart of Jesus. Important figures in Catholic life, especially of France, whole-heartedly espoused the cause. Confraternities were established under this title. Theological works and reviews appeared to stimulate informed thinking on the subject, or guide it within the life of the Church.

Warnings came from Rome against excesses, in the domain of imagery. Despite many requests from bishops for liturgical recognition, despite the fact that St. Pius X, in 1911, enrolled himself as a member of Priests of the Eucharistic Heart of Jesus which he had approved, it was a restrictive decision which emanated in 1914 from the Congregation of Rites, then responsible for public worship. There seemed to be contradiction in its directives with the position officially taken in the *Raccolta*, the approved collection of indulgenced prayers; apparent contradiction also with the Papal Brief by which Leo XIII, 16 February 1903 had approved the Archconfraternity of the Eucharistic Heart of Jesus. Further clarification made it clear that the devotion was approved; but as yet no liturgical ceremony was sanctioned.

The change came on 9 November 1921, when the Congregation of Rites approved a Mass and Office for a feast in honour of the Eucharistic Heart of Jesus; it would be celebrated on the Thursday after the octave of Corpus Christi.

(iii)

Devotion to the Eucharistic Heart of Jesus is of paramount importance at the present time. It serves as a shield against regrettable denial of the divinity of Christ, of his real presence in the Eucharist, of his ardent love for humankind. Faith is strengthened, grows to greater purity by exercise; faith in the divinity of Christ is the rock on which the Christian religion rests. To honour his Heart in the Eucharist is to open the way to total commitment to his divine plan. Here is the highest motivation for trust in his love.

Seen thus the Eucharist assumes for the Christian, for each one who follows Christ, its sublime meaning as a gift, and a gift is essentially from person to person. The Eucharist has a social significance that is immeasurable in a practising community. It raises the level of morality because it creates a common, high motivation.

But it is essentially a gift to a human person, from One who is divine. A gift is most generous when it comes from the Heart. The true response is known to the heart. Here is the explanation of the Sacred Heart's call that reparation be offered to the great Sacrament; here, he made it clear to St. Margaret Mary, he feels most painfully "the ingratitude, the coldness and forgetfulness "hearts who are consecrated" to him.

Here then is the moment to answer a question universally relevant but particularly poignant in regard to the Eucharistic Heart of Jesus: since we believe that Jesus Christ rose from the dead, ascended to the right hand of the Father, is therefore enthroned in glory, how can we speak of him as suffering? A kindred question is, How does the Saviour who is the Lord of history, eliminate the barrier of time and make it possible for us to assist at moments of his earthly life long since consigned to past history?

God the Son entered history as a Redeemer, his redemptive vocation to be beneficial to every single human being who would come to him in faith. Though it was fully achieved as he intimated with the words "It is consummated" (Jn 19:30), its effects had to endure as long as there would be human beings in need of redemption. He rose above history in triumph; he consented to remain part of history as Saviour. He drew on the inexhaustible resources of the divinity which made him independent of time to keep the mysteries of his life present to us; every moment of his life was perpetual for he was intrinsically immortal, in contrast to every moment of ours, which disappears into mortality; we are ever preparing our death.

The Church which he founded to channel to us all the wonders and treasures he had acquired for us is rightly called his Mystical Body; he is its Head (Eph 1:22; Col 1:18). In that sublime office he accepts the conditions of his members, taking from them joy and sorrow; his dual existence, glorious at the right hand of the Father, mystical in his Body the Church, serves to maintain the Church through the ages, making possible a continuous service to sinful mankind.

At the heart of the Church is the Eucharist, Jesus himself; in the Eucharist he is Jesus the Jew, embodying all the wealth of the Jewish civilization of the Heart, King of Angels and of men, his royalty especially exercised in love and mercy, of which his Heart is the most perfect symbol.

(iv)

With such thoughts in mind, the reader may relish what Church authorities have said on the subject of the Eucharistic Heart of Jesus. Leo XIII in the Brief approving the Archconfraternity of the Eucharistic Heart of Jesus: "This Archconfraternity bears this name because it expresses the twofold object of the devotion, the cause and the effect, that is the loving Heart of our Lord, Jesus Christ, and the Holy Eucharist, which is its work par excellence."[2] A note in the *Raccolta*, composed by Cardinal Gotti, and attached to a prayer to the Eucharistic Heart, which had been enriched with indulgences by Leo XIII, 17 June 1902, stated that "worship of the Eucharistic Heart of Jesus takes as a special object of veneration, love, gratitude, and mutual appeal the act of supreme love by which the Heart of Jesus instituted the Eucharist and remains with us until the end of time."[3]

Pius XII wrote thus in the Encyclical *Haurietis Aquas*, which has been already quoted: "It is also our dearest wish that all those who glory in the name of Christian and who labour to establish the Reign of Christ in the world, should regard the practice of devotion to the Heart of Jesus as a standard and source of unity, salvation and peace. At the same time, no one must think that this devotion entails any belittlement of the other forms of religious piety whereby the Christian people, under the Church's guidance, honour the divine Redeemer. Far from it. Without any doubt a burning

---

[2] AAS 35, 1902-03, 582.

[3] *Raccolta*, no. 121, 194.

devotion to the Heart of Jesus will cherish and advance our reverence for the august Sacrament of the Altar. For we dare assert — and this is wonderfully borne out by the revelations vouchsafed by Jesus Christ to St. Gertrude and St. Margaret Mary — that only those have a proper understanding of Jesus Christ crucified who have penetrated the mystic secrets of his Heart. Nor is it easy to fathom the might of that love, constrained by which, Christ has given himself to us as the food of our souls, unless we go out of our way to foster the cult of the Eucharistic Heart of Jesus; the which cult, if we may borrow the words of our predecessor of happy memory, Leo XIII, recalls that 'act of supreme love by which our Redeemer, pouring out all the riches of his Heart in his desire to be with us all days even to the end of the world, instituted the adorable Sacrament of the Eucharist.'" The Pope then quotes St. Albert the Great: "For not the least gift of his Heart is the Eucharist, which he bestowed upon us out of the immense charity of his Heart."[4]

The Decree of approval for the feast reads thus: "This new feast has the purpose of commemorating very specially the love of which our Lord Jesus Christ gives us proof in the mystery of the holy Eucharist. Another purpose is to stir the faithful to approach with ever greater confidence the holy Eucharist, to set their souls aflame with the divine love, the source of which our Lord Jesus Christ has in his Heart burning with an indefinite love, which instituted the Holy Eucharist, which loves his disciples and keeps them in his Sacred Heart, since he lives and dwells in them as they dwell in him, he, who through the Eucharist, offers and gives himself to each one of us, in his quality of victim, companion in exile, food, viaticum, and finally, pledge of heaven."[5]

In the Eucharist as Sacrament, the faithful have the greatest gift they could receive, the "Body and Blood, Soul and Divinity" of Jesus Christ. The Sacred Heart of Jesus is in that gift; he is himself the giver. In the Eucharist as sacrifice the Sacred Heart renews for his faithful the entire Paschal Mystery, Agony, Passion, Death, Resurrection. Again, the Sacred Heart is there on the altar and it is he who, through his priest, performs the sacrifice.

---

[4] *Haurietis Aquas*, CTS.
[5] AAS 13(1921) 545.

(v)

Priests are intrinsically linked with the Eucharist. There is a call to them, in this age of crisis, as in similar moments of the past to fulfill three tasks:

First they have to assimilate into their own lives the true profound meaning of the Sacred Heart of Jesus, origin of the priestly endowment which they bear, source of all their fidelity to their calling. It is in the Sacred Heart that they will see the meaning of service; therein they will touch the mystery of the One who gave them this example, who said that he had come "not to be served, but to serve" (Mk. 10:45). The fervent priest will learn that the service involves giving "his life a ransom for many" (ibid.).

Here is the effective answer to the evils and temptations which surround the priest not only as a human person, but especially in the very office he holds, clericalism, ambition of a worldly kind, routine performance of sacred duties, the inner flame dead and the coldness, which the Lord mentioned, prevailing.

The priest today is at the centre of the Church's crisis and the Eucharist is the centre of the Church's life. For many who fail it is here at the centre that the trouble begins.

We cannot be simplistic in such matters. A profound evil which is reported from many places in the Church in our time is the breakdown in faith, faith that is in the Real Presence of Jesus Christ, true God and true man in the Eucharist. Priests openly admit their loss of faith, sometimes seeking to cover it with a show of theological modernity. It is theology utterly valueless, and the history put forward to support it is equally false.

The second task awaiting the priest is to lead the faithful by instruction and example. They are not totally dependent on him, but concerted belief and practice between them, enlightened by true doctrine contributes to the building of the Mystical Body of Christ.

The faithful can survive without this help from the priest; sometimes they save the day. We may recall the name of Newman who maintained that in the worst doctrinal crisis in the history of the Church, fourth century Arianism, it was the laity who stood firm. In places at the present time where the priest is wavering, the flock are resolute. Priests may here learn from the laity. This, in practical terms, is the People of God, the basic concept of Vatican II, manifest and loyal.

Lastly the priest has to be ready to defend Eucharistic doctrine against heretics and to explain it to those Christians separated from us who do not share our belief. A comforting factor for Catholic priests in this ecumenical age is the strong Eucharistic faith, expressed in beautiful liturgies, of the Orthodox Churches. Here they are today gaining enormously from the overwhelming role of tradition in their outlook, in the life of their Churches.

What an onerous, what a consoling duty belief in the Eucharistic Heart of Christ lays upon the shoulders of all priests and people.

Chapter IV
The Immaculate Heart of Mary

(i)

Pius XII may introduce this subject: "And in order that still more abundant blessings may attend the Christian flock and the entire human race, the faithful should ensure that, to devotion to the Most Sacred Heart of Jesus, they closely unite devotion to the Immaculate Heart of the Mother of God. It was the will of God that, in the accomplishment of man's Redemption, the most blessed Virgin Mary should be inseparably associated with Christ, with the result that our salvation has proceeded from the love and sufferings of Jesus Christ intimately linked with the love and sorrows of his Mother. When, therefore, the faithful, to whom divine life has come from Christ through Mary, have given due worship to the Most Sacred Heart of Jesus, it is altogether fitting that they should honour the most loving Heart of their heavenly Mother with a corresponding expression of loyalty, love, gratitude, and reparation. In perfect harmony, with the most wise and loving design of God's Providence, is that memorable act of consecration by which we ourselves solemnly dedicated God's holy Church and the entire world to the Immaculate Heart of the Blessed Virgin Mary."[1]

This is the first formal statement on the Heart of Mary in a papal Encyclical. As Pius XII said, he had consecrated the human race and the Church to the Immaculate Heart of Mary, on 31 October, 1942; ten years later, in the Encyclical *Sacro Vergente Anno*, addressed to the Russian people, he renewed the consecration for them. This action was, without doubt, related to Fatima, and the messages received there in 1917, amplified later to the sole survivor in 1929.

---

[1] *Haurietis Aquas*, CTS tr.

Let us leave controversy on this subject for the moment and recall some history. But let us first ponder the words of Pius XII: "To you and to your Immaculate Heart in this tragic hour of human history, we commit, we entrust, we consecrate, not only the whole Church, the Mystical Body of your Jesus which suffers and bleeds in so many places, and is afflicted in so many ways, but also the entire world torn by discord, scorched in a fire of hate, victim of its own iniquities.

Since Fatima and its sequel in papal action brought the Immaculate Heart of Mary to public thought that thus it all began. The origins are very much earlier. As has already been stated, there is a reference to the Heart of Mary in the infancy narrative of Luke, "Mary kept all these things pondering them in her Heart" (Lk 2:19; 2:51). This is very much in agreement with the mentality of the Old Testament, the treasury of a civilization of the heart.

(ii)

In patristic and medieval writings, occasional texts have been found which designate her spirit, the centre of her personality, from which response to divine things came, where the Holy Spirit works, wherein she cooperated in salvation, wherein lie treasures of grace for men. Thus Richard of St. Laurent (d. after 1245) writes: "From the heart of the Virgin went forth faith and consent, the two things by which the salvation of the world was begun."[2] "The Holy Spirit," says Godfrey of Admont (d. 1168) "has placed and gathered in the stainless Heart of the Virgin Mary all the elements of healing grace, that is all the gifts of compassion and reconciliation. Thus as there are in the human race illnesses of great variety, springing from weaknesses, this Heart contains also numerous and varied remedies to bring health and healing to souls that are sick."[3]

These quotations show that thought of the Heart of Mary was not strange to some medieval writers. The first prayer addressed directly to the Immaculate Heart was composed about 1184 by the Benedictine Abbot Ekbert of Schoenau, brother of the mystic, Eliza-

---

[2] *De Laudibus S.M.* (*Inter op. Alberti Magni*, ed. Borgnet) 36,2,2,2,p. 82.
[3] *Hom. in Assumpt.*, 7, in PL 174, 986.

beth of Schoenau. It opens thus: "I shall speak to your Heart O Mary. I shall speak to your pure Heart, Mistress of the world, and I shall adore at the holy temple of God, from the most profound depths of my soul. From deep within me I shall salute your Immaculate Heart which first beneath the sun was found worthy to welcome the Son of God, coming forth from the bosom of the Father." The prayer ends thus: "Let every soul magnify you, O Mother of sweetness, and the tongues of all the devout praise the happiness of your Heart whence our salvation flowed." Ekbert used figurative language, recalling the Ark of Sanctification. He enunciates a profound truth in one line: "Hail, unique Sanctuary, which God sanctified to himself in the Holy Spirit."[4]

(iii)

A very notable advance was made in the seventeenth century by St. John Eudes (d. 1680) — this can be said without minimizing the personal contribution in the thirteenth century monastery of Helfta by St. Mechtild of Hackeborn (d. 1298) and St. Gertrude the Great (d. 1302). St. John's success was due to the fact that he celebrated the first Mass in honour of the Heart of Mary, on 8 May, 1648, and composed the first substantial work on *The Admirable Heart of Mary*. His ideas were given a certain permanence through the two religious societies which he founded; a third would also claim him as its inspirer. The saint had dedicated, at Coutances in 1655 and at Caen in 1664, the first churches in the world under the patronage of Mary's Heart.

It is in St. John's book that we shall look for doctrine. He analyses different meanings of the word "heart;" especially he relates the Heart of Mary to each of the divine Persons.

(iv)

We come to the nineteenth century. A remarkable sermon was preached at this time by a Jesuit, Irish-born, living in France, Nicolas

---

[4] H. Barre, C.S.Sp., *Une priere d'Ekbert de Schoenau au Saint Coeur de Marie*, in EphMar 2(1952), 412.

Tuite de McCarthy (d. 1833). His sermon was preached at a time when Marian doctrine and piety were coming out of the pitiful decline which marked the end of the eighteenth century. As a child he had been brought from his native Dublin to escape persecution; he lived through the French Revolution, and saw the Catholic revival which was so signally marked by the manifest power of Our Lady; and she chose to show her power through her Heart.[5]

Fr. de McCarthy preached his sermon for the first time in 1829; the text appeared in the second volume of his sermons issued in 1840; it should be read with two others, one on devotion to Mary, the second on the greatness of Mary. The eloquent preacher deals with the objections made to devotion to Mary. He moves easily through the centuries, always evoking biblical texts stressing the testimony of the Fathers, noting such significant events as the victory of Lepanto, attributed to Our Lady by the reigning Pope, the consecration of France to Mary by Louis XIII, Mary as Protectress of the royal house.

The reader of these thoughtful, well-informed pages will approach his sermon on the Heart of Mary with respectful curiosity. Not many were at the time dealing at length oratorically with the theme — nor willing to publish their texts. He prays for divine help: "O Mother of the Saviour, how can we worthily praise your Heart, if you do not deign yourself to open to us this sanctuary of all the virtues, the living temple of the Holy Spirit, that we may contemplate the riches which it encloses, and making them known to our listeners we should fill them with admiration, thankfulness and love for the most perfect and beneficent of all hearts after that of Jesus."

The original plan of God was thwarted by the sin of Adam. But "preserved from the universal corruption by a miracle of grace, a daughter of Adam is conceived in innocence and is born in holiness. In her the Lord sees all beauty, all the purity of the first de-

---

[5] Quotations from *Sermons du R.P. de McCarthy*, Lyons, Paris, 1840, vol. II; there are critical problems, as to whether the sermons were based on his papers, but the essentials were his; cf. H. de Gennac in D SP, X 46-47; two disciples of the Heart of Mary to be mentioned shortly apparently heard Fr. de McCarthy: Abbe Dufriche-Desgenettes was not impressed. Francis Libermann apparently may have heard the preacher and learned from him, cf. infra.

sign on which he had formed man come to life again. Oh, with what joy he contemplates this Heart which no stain disfigures, no seed of passion soils, which not even the lightest fault will ever render less worthy of his love; this Heart, all of whose tendencies are holy and all its affections are heavenly!, or rather with what satisfaction he contemplates therein himself as in a faithful mirror, finding therein all the features of his likeness which have been effaced in all others."

The preacher exhausts his noble rhetoric in praise of the virtues of this Heart. He pauses to exclaim: "But what, Lord, have I taken on? Have I believed that in a single discourse, I could praise all the perfections of the Heart of Mary? Did I have a hundred tongues and a hundred voices, could I even name them? Is this sacred Heart not a depthless abyss of virtues and wonders?"

Fr. de McCarthy reflects on the relationship between the Heart of Mary, centre of her whole being and each of the divine Persons: "The Father adopted, in a very special manner, as his daughter, the one who would be the Spouse of his Spirit and the Mother of his only Son. He preserved her alone from the original sin, sanctified not only her birth but her very conception, and prepared her, from her mother's womb, by an outpouring of graces unexampled and without measure; before she was born she could already have been called full of grace as truthfully as Gabriel did: *Gratia plena*...There in this Heart the sacred fire does not go out, where there burns ceaselessly an incense of pleasant odour; there is the true altar of holocausts where the pure victim is immolated and consumed constantly; the true Holy of Holies, where the Eternal One secretly gives out his oracles; and the living Ark, of which that of the Hebrews was but a figure."

Then the great preacher turns to Mary and the Holy Spirit, a theme very actual in the most responsible thinking within the Catholic Church since Vatican II. Let us listen to Fr. de McCarthy: "It is there also, it is in this virginal Heart that the ineffable wedding of the Spirit will be celebrated. Come down O Divine Spirit, the spouse is ready, she is adorned with chastity, humility, love, with all the variety and magnificence of the virtues which for her form the richest wedding dress, one most worthy of you: *In vestitu deaurato, circumdata varietate* (Ps 44:10). Come to accomplish in her the prodigy awaited for centuries, this mystery incomprehensible even to the angels, which is to unite her to you by unbreakable links, and give her a title and rights which it did not seem possible that a creature could ever claim."

The preacher develops this thought at great length, comparing the Spirit's descent on Mary with that on the Apostles, as he elaborates splendidly the intimate relationship with her divine Son. He cannot understand those who are willing to applaud the different honours given to Mary, but who will not tolerate special veneration for her Heart. He dismesses such a minimalist attitude.

When Fr. McCarthy comes to speak of Mary's love for us, he shows how this love was co-redemptive: "*Stabat juxta crucem Jesu mater ejus* (Jn 19:25). What does she do? While Jesus offers himself to his Father for the expiation of our sins, his Mother offers him also for the same purpose: she consents to his torment, to his ignominies, to his death, that we should obtain grace; she entreats a God who is offended to appease his vengeance on this innocent Lamb, and to spare us. See how much the Heart of Mary loved us.....*Mulier ecce filius tuus.* New Eve, behold your family; henceforth only you are the true mother of all the living, that is of my disciples; today you give birth to them in the excess of most inconceivable pain; and finally you accomplish in its full extent the prophecy given to the first woman: *In dolore paries filios* (Gen 3:16).

(v)

In the age of Fr. McCarthy, who exemplifies theological and pastoral reflection, there occurred two singular supernatural events which were to have far-reaching effects. On 27 November, 1830, Catherine Laboure received the revelation of the Miraculous Medal in the Rue du Bac; it was distributed a millionfold throughout the world; to its bearers and beneficiaries it carried the message of the two Hearts.

Just a little over six years later, on 3 December, 1836, the church of Notre Dame des Victoires was the setting. Parish life was moribund and the Cure, Fr. Charles Eleanor Dufriche Desgenettes, oppressed by the decay, had decided to go elsewhere. On that day, after Mass, he heard a voice saying: "Consecrate your parish to the holy and Immaculate Heart of Mary." He found it difficult to accept — thinking of an illusion. He yielded and did as he was told. The first effect was remarkable revival in Catholic practice locally, then the foundation of a confraternity of the Immaculate Heart of Mary, Refuge of Sinners. Pius IX raised it to an Archconfraternity; it spread into many other countries.[6] In 1860, there were twenty million associates.

Notre Dame des Victoires became a popular shrine for clients of Our Lady.[7] It was the scene of a famous encounter with an immense missionary future. A pilgrim there in the early forties was an Irish-American bishop, strictly a Vicar apostolic, Edward Barron, to whom had been assigned a vast stretch of the west coast of Africa. He told Abbe Desgenettes that he had a missionary area but no missionaries. About the same time, a good friend of the Abbe's looked in on him; he mentioned the fact that he had missionaries ready to leave for Africa, but nowhere to send them. The obvious agreement was reached.[8]

Venerable Francis Libermann deserves more than a passing mention. A convert Jew, he had "detested" the Blessed Virgin before he became a Catholic. In the moment of Baptism, he had a unique mystical experience. Thereafter he was totally devout to Our Lady, her Holy Heart the centre of his piety. He chose it as the patronal title of his society for the black race. To the Immaculate Heart of Mary, Bishop Barron had also consecrated his vast mission; on the east of Africa some time later a similar act was performed. Of Libermann's first seven missionaries accompanying the Bishop, six died quickly and the seventh was lost. His own first bishop, Mgr. Truffet, died ten months after reaching Senegal. The lion-hearted founder did not surrender to disaster. The African mission born of the Heart of Mary arose triumphant out of every ordeal, is today, after a century and a quarter, the greatest success

---

[6] On Abbe Dufriche-Desgennettes, cf. J. Letourneur in D Sp, III, 1757-59.

[7] St. Therese of Lisieux tells of her visit to the shrine and the reassurance she received of Our Lady's intervention to heal her from illness.

[8] On Francis Libermann cf. P. Sigrist in D Sp IX, 764-780; Paul Coulon, Paule Bram, ed. Libermann, Paris, 1988; Henry Koren, C.S.Sp. *To the Ends of the Earth*, Pittsburgh, 1983, pp. 166-265.

story in evangelization over the last thousand years: one hundred million Catholics, eight million in Nigeria.

(vi)

Before leaving the nineteenth century, there is another name to add. Few people know that the great Newman, the imperial intellect of his age, a future Doctor of the Church in the opinion of Pius XII, found a special place in his spirituality for the Sacred Heart of Jesus. This led him logically to the kindred devotion to the Immaculate Heart of Mary. It is known that he wore a Miraculous Medal for some time before becoming a Catholic. We have his ideas, his hopes and his pleas in the beautiful series of invocations, which make up his Litany in honour of the Immaculate Heart of Mary.[9]

(vi)

So we come to our own crisis-wracked century and to Fatima. The story is generally well known. Let us concentrate on what the great history of the mighty drama, Fr. Joaquin Alonso, C.M.F., has said is "its soul:" the Immaculate Heart of Mary. Let us look at exact texts, first that which records what happened on the third apparition of Our Lady on 13 July, 1917. "(The Blessed Virgin) went on. Would you sacrifice yourself for sinners and say often especially each time you make a sacrifice: O Jesus it is for your love, for the conversion of sinners and in reparation for the sins committed against the Immaculate Heart of Mary (then follows the story of the vision of hell);

"You have seen hell where the souls of poor sinners go. In order to save them, God wants to establish in the world devotion to my Immaculate Heart. If people do what I shall tell you, many souls will be saved and peace will come. The war is going to finish but if people do not stop offending God, another war, worse this time, will begin in the pontificate of Pius XI. When you see a certain night lit up by an unknown light, you will know that it is the great sign God is giving to you that he is going to punish the world

---

[9]   We shall return to Newmann in a later chapter.

for its crimes by means of war, famine and persecution against the Church and the Holy Father. To prevent it I shall come and ask for the consecration of Russia to my Immaculate Heart and for the Communion of reparation of first Saturdays. If my requests are listened to, Russia will be converted and you will have peace. If not, Russia will spread her errors throughout the world, provoking wars and persecutions against the Church. Good people will be martyred. The Holy Father will suffer much. Several nations will be annihilated. Finally, my Immaculate Heart will triumph. The Holy Father will consecrate Russia to me and it will be converted, and a certain period of peace will be given to the world. The dogmas of the faith will be preserved in Portugal. Do not tell this to anyone. You can only tell it to Francis."[10]

The recipient of this divine communication, Lucy, was subsequently a member of the sisters of St. Dorothy in Spain, in Pontevedra. There she had special divine favours. One was crucial. Her own words:

"It was during the time that Our Lord informed me that the moment had come when he wanted me to make known to Holy Church his desire for the consecration of Russia, and his promise to convert her. He communicated this to me in the following manner:

"I had asked for and obtained permission from my Superiors to make a Holy Hour from 11 p.m. to midnight during the night of Thursday-Friday. Being alone one night, I knelt down at the middle of the balustrade which is in the centre of the chapel, to recite prostrate the prayers of the angel. Feeling tired, I got up and continued to recite them with arms outstretched. The only light was that of the sanctuary lamp. Suddenly the whole chapel lit up as by a supernatural light, and there appeared on the altar a Cross of light which rose up as far as the ceiling. In this very clear light one could see on the upper part of the Cross the figure of a man from the waist upwards and upon his chest was a dove also luminous. Nailed to the Cross was another man. A little below his waist suspended in the air one could see a chalice and a large host upon which there fell several drops of blood, which flowed upon the

---

[10] Reproduced by Fr. Alonso in *A Heart for All*, Washington, 1972, p. 25f.

cheeks of the crucified one, and from a wound on his chest. Flowing over the host, these drops fell into the chalice.

"Under the right arm of the cross was Our Lady (It was Our Lady of Fatima with her Immaculate Heart in her left hand without sword or roses, but with a crown of thorns and flames).

"Under the left arm of the cross large letters of crystalline water which had flowed over the altar and formed these words, 'Grace and Mercy.'

"I understood that the mystery of the most holy Trinity had been shown to me, and I received enlightenment upon this mystery which is not permitted to me to reveal.

"Then Our Lady said to me: 'The time has come for God to ask the Holy Father to make, in union with all the bishops of the world, the consecration of Russia to my Immaculate Heart. He promises to save Russia by this means. They are so numerous these sins that the justice of God condemns and which are committed against me, that I have come to ask for reparation. Sacrifice yourself for this intention and pray.'

"I gave an account of this to my confessor, and he asked me to write down what our Lord wanted to be done.

"Later on, through an intimate communication, Our Lord complained: 'They have not chosen to heed my request!..., As the King of France, they will regret it, and then will do it but it will be very late. Russia will already have spread her errors into the world, provoking wars and persecutions against the Church. The Holy Father will have much to suffer."[11]

Sister Lucy had this vision and revelation on a date between the 11th and 13th June, 1929. The Holy See was informed of this heavenly request in a memorandum sent in March, 1937 by Dom Jose da Silva, Bishop of Leiria, the diocese which includes Fatima. Nothing happened. In 1940, Sister Lucy sent a letter to Pius XII, whittling down to some extent the original request of Our Lady, but asking for the consecration to the Immaculate Heart of Mary — there had been those who did not think the full request should be made.

---

[11] *Ibid.*, pp. 34-38.

(vii)

Pius XII was consecrated bishop on 13 May, 1917; he was a Marian Pope. Yet, for two years he made no response to Our Lady. On 31 October, 1942, broadcasting to Portugal for the Silver Jubilee of the apparitions, he included these words in his discourse: "To You, to your Immaculate Heart, We, as universal father of the great Christian family, as Vicar of him to whom you have given all power over heaven and earth, and from whom we have received the care of all souls, redeemed by his blood, who inhabit the world, to You, to your Immaculate Heart, in this tragic hour of human history, we entrust, we offer, we consecrate, not only Holy Church, the Mystical Body of your Son, Jesus, which suffers and bleeds in so many places and in so many ways, but also the whole world, torn by mortal strife, ablaze with hate, and victim of its own sins."

There was an oblique reference to Russia: "To the peoples separated by error or dissension, especially those who profess a special devotion to You, and with whom there is not a house which does not honour your holy icon (perhaps today hidden and kept for better days), give peace and lead them back to be one fold of Christ, under the one true Shepherd..."[12]

On the 7th July, 1952, Pius XII published an Apostolic Letter, *Sacro Vergente Anno*, addressed to the Russian people. The Pope stated that many had told him of their joy at his definition of the Dogma of the Assumption — the date was November 1, 1950. He went on: "Certain of those who have sent us letters of congratulation have also requested us with fervour to consecrate to the Immaculate Heart of Mary the entire Russian nation, which is in a state of anguish. The request greatly pleased us... Consequently, in order that our prayers and supplications, as well as yours, would be more readily granted, and in order to give you special proof of our good will for many years, we have consecrated the entire human race to the Immaculate Heart of the Virgin, Mother of God, thus now we entrust and consecrate in a very special way to the Immaculate Heart of Mary, all the peoples of Russia in the utmost confidence that the wishes which we express keep a true peace,

---

[12] *Our Lady, Papal Teachings*, ed. Solesmes, English tr. Boston, 343.

fraternal harmony, freedom for all, and above all for the Church, that all of these soon become a sweet reality, thanks to the all-powerful help and the patronage of the Virgin Mary."

A question must be faced, painful for one like the present writer who so admires Pius XII, has defended him over the years in regard to his action on behalf of the threatened Jews: Did Pius XI and Pius XII fail Our Lady? If the consecration of Russia in union with all the bishops had been made before World War II, would the conversion of Russia have begun and much evil been avoided?

Some recent history is interesting. On 13 May, 1981, John Paul II was struck down by an assassin's bullets; in convalescence he learned much about Our Lady of Fatima. On the anniversary, 13 May, 1982, he went to thank her. He pronounced a lengthy prayer, which was not the desired consecration. On 25 March, 1984, in Rome, before a statue brought from Fatima, having previously informed the bishops of the Church, he read an act of universal consecration — but without naming Russia!

(viii)

Let us, however, hear the Pope's words: "Behold, as we stand before you, Mother of Christ, before your Immaculate Heart, we desire, together with the whole Church, to unite ourselves with the consecration which, for love of us, your Son made of himself to the Father. 'For their sake,' he said, 'I consecrate myself that they also may be consecrated in the truth' (Jn. 17:19). We wish to unite ourselves with our Redeemer in this, his consecration for the world and for the human race, which in his divine Heart, has the power to obtain pardon and to secure reparation.

"The power of this consecration lasts for all time, and embraces all individuals, peoples, and nations. It overcomes every evil that the spirit of darkness is able to awaken, and has in fact awakened in our times, in the heart of man and in his history...

"Hail to you, who are wholly united to the redeeming consecration of your Son.

"Mother of the Church! Enlighten the People of God along the paths of faith, hope, and love! Enlighten especially the peoples whose consecration and entrustment by us you are awaiting. Help us to live in the truth of the consecration of Christ for the entire human family of the modern world.

"In entrusting to you, O Mother of the world, all individuals and peoples, we also entrust to you this very consecration of the world, placing it in your motherly Heart."[13]

The redeemer may compare with this formula of consecration that of 13 May, 1982, printed in Appendix; there is a close resemblance between them. The surviving witness of Fatima, Sister Lucy, now a Carmelite nun in Coimbra, is quoted as a guarantor of the request made by Our Lady. She did not think that the 1982 prayer met the demand; that of 1984, she thought, did.

Before the second act of consecration, the Pope had on 8 December, 1983, informed the world's Catholic and Orthodox bishops of his intention, asking them to join him. Thus was fulfilled one condition prescribed by Our Lady. When the Bishop of Fatima, Mgr. Alberto Cosme de Amaral, thanked him after the ceremony for consecrating the world, John Paul II replied, "And Russia!" It was therefore his intention and we must believe that he had Russia especially in mind when he spoke of "the peoples whose consecration and entrustment by us you are awaiting."

On more than one occasion Sister Lucy has stated that John Paul II had met Our Lady's request. She stated this to a visiting Indian bishop. I beg to add a personal testimony. Those of us celebrating in Fatima the seventy fifth anniversary of the Apparitions in October 1992, were joined by two eminent citizens of the Philippines: Corazon ("Cory") Aquino and Ambassador Howard Dee; he had been her first nominee as Ambassador to the Holy See when she was president of her country. They had come from Coimbra where, with papal permission, they had interviewed Sister Lucy. In answer to the pertinent question to them also she had affirmed her belief that what Our Lady had requested had been done.

---

[13] ORE 1984, 828:9-10. Pius VI allowed a feast of the Immaculate Heart of Mary to Palermo; Pius VII, in 1805, granted it to dioceses and congregations requesting it — the Mass was that of Our Lady of the Snows 5 August. In 1942, Pius XII promoted it to a feast of Double rite, fixing it on 22 August. Recent reform has placed it on the Saturday after the feast of the Sacred Heart, as an optional memorial.

The reader will take these statements as he or she values the role of Sister Lucy. The awkward question remains: Why did John Paul II not name Russia? Only he can answer this question. Comment from anyone else is conjecture. With that proviso, I suggest that the Pope did not wish to add to the tension existing in Russia between the Orthodox and the Catholic minority. By appointing three Catholic bishops, one the Archbishop Kondrociewiecz of Moscow, he had aroused acute opposition. The Russian Orthodox were apprehensive about what they deemed proselytism, a policy of drawing their faithful into the Catholic Church. They resent uniatism, that is the existence of eastern rite Christians united with the Church of Rome.

John Paul II is the Pope of the Orthodox. None of his predecessors in the high office has shown such profound knowledge of Orthodoxy, has made such efforts to achieve mutual understanding with these great Churches of the East. He expressed his insights in the Apostolic Letter *Orientale Lumen*, unequaled in papal documents. Almost week by week he speaks of some aspect of Orthodox theology or devotion. Annually, he sends a delegation to the Ecumenical Patriarch in Istanbul, welcomes in Rome one from the Patriarch. With Dimitrios I (d. 1991), he set up a joint Catholic Orthodox theological commission; in June, 1993, they produced an epoch-making declaration, from Balamand in the Lebanon on the vexed problems of the Churches. A high moment in Catholic Orthodox relations was the encounter in Rome for the feast of SS Peter and Paul, 1995 of the Ecumenical Patriarch Bartholomew I and the Pope; the pronouncements were deeply significant.

(ix)

All this and so much more must be borne in mind when the Pope's act of consecration on 25 March, 1984, is judged. But we have a right to ask a further question: If the consecration was valid, did the promised result follow? Have we seen the beginning of the conversion of Russia? Again I offer a personal testimony. As a practising journalist I visited the country twice, in 1966 briefly on my own, and in 1968 with fellow journalists from the International Catholic Press Congress, which had taken place in Berlin. In 1966, I could not say Mass; in 1968, I did celebrate the Holy Sacrifice, with a fellow journalist, Fr. Michael Traber, then working in Northern Rhodesia, now Zimbabwe; it was in the private apartment of a priest registered as a member of an embassy.

In 1992, with the American Catholic 101 Foundation, I was back in Moscow. Our visit coincided with the International Catholic Youth Congress taking place in the Cosmos Hotel — this event was publicised in the lobbies and on the stairways of the hotel. I was able to concelebrate Mass with fifty priests and five bishops in the hotel auditorium. When members of our party went into the streets offering religious emblems, people vied to get them.

Did Our Lady attract attention? Her statue was borne from the plane to the airport terminal with a guard of honour composed of priests and bishops, airport personnel and security officers respectfully attentive. This statue was crowned on Red Square. The well-informed told us that the statue had been brought into the city, over the Kremlin, on the anniversary of the day that St. Maximilian Kolbe had, in his prison cell in Auschwitz, foretold the event.

Aspects of the whole religious revival are well known. The visit to the Pope by the head of state was more than symbolic, as he invited John Paul II to visit Moscow, promised a charter of religious freedom which has been enacted and mutual diplomatic representation. The churches inside the Kremlin, of the Annunciation, the Assumption of Our Lady and St. Michael have been restored to religious worship; they had been treated as museums; the two most beautiful icons, of Our Lady of Vladimir, and of the Holy Trinity — Rublev's masterpiece, are no longer museum pieces. Religious statistics indicate continuous recovery and growth.

Since we are speaking of the effects of a papal act of consecration a noteworthy tribute has come from a high Russian source: the great change was facilitated by the presence of a Slav citizen in the Chair of Peter.[14]

---

[14] The Pope's invitation to the world's bishops ensured the collegial character of his act. After the consecration, before a statue of Our Lady brought from the Capelhina and placed outside St. Peter's in Rome, Sister Lucia was interviewed by the Nuncio in Portugal. "Is Russia now consecrated?" he asked. "Yes, now it is," she replied. The Nuncio said, "Now we wait for the miracle." She said, "Yes, God will keep his word." cf. *Fatima Family Messenger*, Oct/Dec 1989, p.7.

[1] Participants in the symposium were: Sacred Scripture, Fr. Ingace de la Potterie, S.J., of the Biblical Institute; Patrology, Fr. Domiciano Fernandez, C.M.F., editor, *Ephemerides Mariologicae*; Middle Ages, Fr. Theodore Koehler, S.M., distinguished Marian theologian, professor and librarian, University of Dayton, Ohio; Seventeenth Century, Rev. Arthur Burton Calkins, specialist in the period, and in papal teaching; Nineteenth and Twentieth Century, Rev. Michael O'Carroll, C.S.Sp.; Teaching Authority of the Church, Fr. Rene Laurentin; Mystical Theology, Fr. Candido Pozo, S.J., of the Gregorian University; Liturgy, Fr. Anscar J. Chupungco, O.S.B., Pontifical Liturgical Institute, Rome; Systematic Theology, Fr. Christoph von Schoenborn, O.P., then Professor at Fribourg University. The Pontifical Marian Academy, through its president, Fr. Paolo Melada, O.F.M., gave the organising committee the hospitality of its rooms in Rome; Fr. Melada was invited to chair the symposium meetings in Fatima.

Chapter V
The Two Hearts

(i)

The phrase "Alliance of the Two Hearts" was first used by Pope John Paul II in a catechesis in September, 1985. It was taken up in the Philippines where a number of influential Catholics decided to make it the subject of a symposium to which important theologians were invited. Fatima was chosen as the venue, the time September, 1986; prominent Filipinos were Cardinal Sin and Fr. Catalino Arevalo, S.J. of the Manila Ateneo, and Ambassador Howard Dee. Mr. John Haffert, of the Blue Army, now the World Fatima Apostolate; his association helped materially.

The steering committee charged with organisation had a pleasant surprise. They approached theologians of stature. In view of the decline which had been noticed in the Church of Marian theology and piety — it was described at Huelva during the International Mariological Congress in 1972 as a "decade without Mary," some might have wished to keep away. No one refused. One was the author of the remark just quoted, the biblical scholar, Fr. Ignace de la Potterie, S.J. The plan of lectures was ambitious, covering everything from Sacred Scripture through the distinctive periods of history to modern times, then featuring general themes like the Liturgy, Mystical Theology, the Teaching Authority, a final theological synthesis. Internationally known names like Rene Laurentin and Christoph von Schonborn, O.P. were a certain guarantee of doctrinal integrity.[1]

Still more so was the direct interest of the Pope. It is not often that a papal Letter is sent to the participants in a symposium. This document we were privileged to receive through the intermediary of Cardinal Sin. Moreover, the Pope invited the participants in the symposium to meet him in Rome at the conclusion of their work.

---

[1] √ See Previous Page.

They presented to him the proceedings, that is the entire documents submitted and discussed at the meetings. They added a Votum that the Holy Father would issue an official pronouncement based on their research and findings. This was not done, possibly because the Pope had in hand the Encyclical he was shortly to publish, on Our Lady, *Redemptoris Mater*. His continuing interest in the theme has been more than once manifest. To a congress on the Alliance of the Two Hearts held in Dublin in September, 1993, the Pope sent a special message. In May 1994, he invited to concelebrate with him in his private oratory Filipino Bishops and theologians taking part in the Rome congress on the Alliance of the Two Hearts. Meeting the participants afterwards he was heard to say, "The Philippines have begun this great movement, seeking theologians in Europe."

Why have congresses of this kind taken place in different countries; why should we hope for an increasing, widespread number of them? Before looking at the proceedings of the Fatima symposium, let us recall some interesting facts. The miraculous Medal has been mentioned. Let us return to Fatima. In the year before the great, well-known apparitions, the children who were to be the privileged witnesses, had three times an apparition of the Angel of Peace, of their country. On each occasion the heavenly visitor spoke to them of the Hearts of Jesus and Mary.

(ii)

Let us look at a letter of Sister Lucy, written on 18 May, 1936: "As to the other question, if it is fitting to insist upon the consecration of Russia, I reply in almost the same way as before. I regret that it has not been done; but God himself who has asked for it has, therefore, permitted it. If it is fitting to insist I do not know. It seems to me that if the Holy Father did it now, Our Lord would accept it and would fulfill his promise and without any doubt it would, therefore, please Our Lord and the Immaculate Heart of Mary. I have spoken in an intimate manner on this subject to Our Lord and a short time ago I asked him why he would not convert Russia without the consecration by His Holiness. 'Because,' (Our Lord said), 'I want all the Church to recognise this consecration as a triumph of the Immaculate Heart of Mary so that this devotion will then be extended, and to place devotion to this Immaculate Heart beside the devotion to my divine Heart.' 'But, my God,' (I said, 'the Holy Father will not believe me if you do not move me yourself by a special inspiration.' Oh, the Holy Father! Pray very much for the Holy Father. He will do it, but this will be very late. However, the Immaculate Heart of Mary will save Russia; it is entrusted to her."[2]

(iii)

When we look into the deep reasons which explain the union between the two Hearts we must consider the entire plan of salvation. The Heart of Jesus, unique source of our salvation and sanctification, came into our world through an act of the Heart of Mary. Without her consent in the moment of the Annunciation, God would not have become man; that consent came from her whole Heart. In that moment was made, by the Holy Spirit, a mysterious, utterly unbreakable, bond which will last forever. These two Hearts were one, as no others could be. Mary, the Virgin, gave the Incarnate Word the Heart of flesh which he will show as the perfect symbol of his love for all of us. It is a unity as near to total identity as could be, safeguarding the separate existence of each.

From this point of origin came the overwhelming concentration of power which we may contemplate in the two Hearts. The Heart of a perfect man, strong, resourceful, inspiring, daring was one with the Heart of a perfect woman, infinitely patient, utterly tender, delicate, courageous.

Who is the author of this unity? Here we enter a vast, compelling subject which would take volumes; on the neglect of the Holy Spirit in the Catholic Church, until the fourth session of the Second Vatican Council, neglect not attributable to all, scarcely to Pius XII, certainly to his immediate predecessors, as to the Catholic Hierarchy in general, and, with a few exceptions, to teachers, that is theologians, and preachers. During the decades preceding Vatican II, who can recall a single sermon on the Holy Spirit? To how many thinking of speaking on the Holy Spirit, especially on the Gifts of

---

[2]   Apud Joaquin Maria Alonso, op.cit., p. 55f.

the Spirit has the stricture been applied, "that is Theology, you cannot speak of that to an ordinary congregation." Why did not one single Bishop, the spokesman for one single university faculty, in their submissions on a possible agenda for Vatican II, not mention the Holy Spirit? The obvious justification would be made: church dogma on the Holy Spirit is complete, since the Council of Constantinople in 381 A.D.

But Vatican II was a pastoral council, attentive allegedly, to stirrings of grace among the faithful. Were the Council Fathers unaware of the vast movement centred on the Spirit, charismatic in its title? Did they not see the need to offer conciliar guidance to their faithful so generously committed?

Vatican II was, by its intention and its procedure, ecumenical. Did the Fathers not see the need to speak to the Orthodox on a subject most dear to them, the Holy Spirit? They were reminded of their duty towards the end of the third session, in an article which will be quoted indefinitely. Nikos Nissiotis, a scholarly Greek theologian, rector of the Bossey Institute run by the World Council of Churches, editor of the organ of this body, *The Ecumenical Review*, published in this periodical his article which in effect said that if the Father of Vatican II did not speak of the Holy Spirit in their documents, these would have no effect in the Orthodox Church.

We enter thereon a debate which would take us far afield: Did Vatican II give a teaching on the Holy Spirit? Are there not two hundred and fifty eight references to the subject in the conciliar documents? Among these, there are certainly important passages; not all are purely nominal. Yet the need seems to have been felt, for if, for example, one compares what is said about the Mass in the Constitution on the Sacred Liturgy issued in the first session, with what one reads in the Decree on The Ministry and Life of Priests, from the fourth session, the presence of the Holy Spirit is quite evident in the latter, absent in the former.

Pope Paul VI practically admitted the justice of the Nissiotis complaint when he said, after the Council, that to its ecclesiology and Mariology teachers and preachers must now add a theology of the Holy Spirit. Has his recommendation been heeded? Certainly by his successor in the See of Peter. John Paul II is the Pope of the Holy Spirit; he has spoken and written more on the subject than all of his predecessors in the See of Peter taken together.

We are here interested in what the Pope has said about the Spirit in regard to Jesus and Mary. He has in regard to Jesus splendidly interpreted a recent current of thought in Christology: there is no Christology without a theology of the Holy Spirit. Hear John Paul II:

"If previously we have shown the wonders of the Holy Spirit announced by Jesus and experienced at Pentecost and during the initial journey of the Church in history, the time has come to emphasize the fact that the first and greatest wonder accomplished by the Holy Spirit is Christ himself. It is towards this wonder that we want to direct your attention.....In accomplishing the mystery of the Incarnation, there was a decisive presence of the Spirit, to the degree that, if we want to grasp and enunciate this mystery more fully, it is not enough to say that the Word was made flesh; we must also underline — as happens in the Creed — the Spirit's role in forming the humanity of the Son of God in the virginal womb of Mary. We will speak about this later. And we will attempt to follow the Holy Spirit in the life and mission of Christ: in his childhood, in the inauguration of his public life through his Baptism, in his sojourn in the desert, in prayer, in preaching, in sacrifice, and finally, in resurrection.

"A basic truth emerged from examination of the Gospel texts: what Christ was, and what he is for us, cannot be understood apart from the Holy Spirit. That means that not only is the Holy Spirit's light necessary for penetrating Christ's mystery, but the influence of the Holy Spirit in the Incarnation of the Word and in the entire life of Christ must be taken into account to explain the Jesus of the Gospel. The Holy Spirit left the mark of his own personality on the face of Christ.

"Therefore, arriving at a deeper awareness of Christ demands also a deeper awareness of the Holy Spirit. 'To know who Christ is' and 'to know who the Spirit is' are two indissolubly linked requirements, the one implying the other. We can add that even the Christian's relationship with Christ is integrally joined to his or her relationship with the Spirit."[3]

---

[3]   ORE, 1990, April 2.

(iv)

Much has been written through the ages on the relationship between the Holy Spirit and Mary, very much by the present Pope. Vatican II spoke of her as the "sanctuary" of the Spirit, whereas saints like St. Louis Marie Grignion de Montfort and St. Maximilian Kolbe, and Popes Leo XIII, Pius XII and John Paul II speak of her as Spouse of the Holy Spirit. It must be admitted that according to St. Paul every Christian is a sanctuary of the Holy Spirit; Our Lady has a more profound, meaningful relationship with the Sanctifier.

Pope Paul VI expresses the reality thus: "We must consider, therefore, that the activity of the Mother of the Church for the benefit of the redeemed does not replace, or compete with, the almighty and universal action of the Holy Spirit. Rather, the former implores and prepares for the latter, not only by prayer of intercession, in harmony with the divine plans which Mary contemplates in the beatific vision, but also with the direct influence of her example, in particular the extremely important one of her supreme docility to the inspirations of the Divine Spirit. It is, therefore, always in dependence on the Holy Spirit that Mary leads souls to Jesus, forms them in her image, inspires them with good advice and serves as a bond of love between Jesus and the faithful.

"To confirm these reflections, we are happy to recall the testimony of the Fathers and Doctors of the Eastern Church. They are models of belief in and worship of the Holy Spirit; they have also witnessed to the Church's belief in and veneration of the Mother of Christ as the Mediatrix of divine favours....They take it for granted and sometimes expressly declare that the Virgin's meditative activity depends upon and has its source in that of the Spirit of God."[4]

John Paul answers our question on the immediate authorship of the Alliance of the two Hearts. It is the Holy Spirit. In view of what has been recorded in the previous passages his succinct judgement will be illuminating: "We can say that just as the mystery of Redemption began in the womb of the Virgin Mary, so did that

---

[4] AAS 67(1975): p. 358, Letter to Cardinal Suenens, Legate to International Marian Congress.

splendid union of the Hearts of Christ and his Mother. From the very moment when the Word was made flesh beneath the Heart of Mary, there has existed, *under the influence of the Holy Spirit*, an enduring relationship of love between them."

Thus, John Paul II wrote to the Fatima symposium. In his address to the symposium participants whom he received in Rome he spoke these words: "I presented this same thought in my first Encyclical, *Redemptor Hominis*, in which I pointed out that from the first moment of the Redemptive Incarnation 'under the special influence of the Holy Spirit,' Mary's Heart, the Heart of both a virgin and a mother, has always followed the work of her Son and has gone out to all those whom Christ has embraced and continues to embrace with inexhaustible love."

When we think of the Holy Spirit promised to Mary in the moment of the Incarnation, we may have the illusion of a last minute arrival. But the Spirit is a divine Person, interested and active from all eternity in the sublime mystery of the Incarnation, his announcement and his descent eternally planned, that is thought out in loving detail, his decisive, indispensable role of its nature perpetual. The Holy Spirit unites the two Hearts from the moment of the Incarnation, which does not mean that we can totally comprehend his action. Pope Paul VI spoke in *Marialis Cultus* (no. 27) of the "hidden relationship between the Spirit of God and the Virgin of Nazareth." How much more mysterious is that between the Spirit and the Sacred Heart of Jesus, about which Pius XII speaks, as we have seen in *Haurietis Aquas*. How unfathomable then in the two most perfect is the interchange of the Spirit's power and his Gifts.

The Gifts of the Spirit? We learn of them because they have been promised to the Messiah (Is 11:2) and the Church teaches that his followers also receive them. Who more perfectly than his most perfect disciple? Who was equipped and ideally faithful to partake of the spiritual wonders which the Spirit poured into her soul open to that of Jesus as the Spouse of the Spirit? We can ponder how the Gifts stirred to every mutual need between these two perfect ones. To attempt to lay a schematic man-made pattern over the events and words of the Gospel would be not only hazardous, but lacking in the sense of the sacred, itself one of the Gifts we have received.

Can we really enter into communion with these two Hearts as

one, as St. John Eudes encourages us to do? For though mysterious, they touch what is most intimate within us; though transcending our finite nature they are never alien, never remote. They are the ultimate gift of God's generosity to frail, sin-stained humanity. Only God could have thought of this; only God-made man could have realized it.

How are they best approached? Through what they themselves essentially and existentially are, through our hearts — for each one through his or her heart, but heart in its total sense, as the principle of unity in the human person — to borrow an idea from our Orthodox friends.

Newman knew something of this when he took as his motto as Cardinal, *Cor ad cor loquitur*: Heart speaks to heart. Inviting union but holding an unconquerable overwhelming power dominant over every possible evil. In the end of our mishaps, calamities and of every project mounted against us by the evil one, these two Hearts will triumph.

(v)

The stirrings and movement of Mary's Heart were responsive to the Heart of her divine Son in a way unexampled, for every fibre of his being matched, reflected hers uniquely. There was in his physique, in the intimate structure of his nature, a similarity to her that made communion of heart between them sensitive and meaningful as it had never existed or could exist between two human beings: her virginal motherhood, her flesh given to form him by her consent, kept her presence to him perpetual.

Theologians have the duty of explaining Mary's role in the lifework, the mission and the achievement of her divine Son. Attention is particularly given at this moment in many centres to her titles of Co-Redemptress, Mediatress and Advocate. To pursue their studies here would take us far afield. It may be said that when the final outcome of the current research and reasoning has been reached, it will manifest a deep harmony between the experience of the faithful, the work of theologians and the Church's Teaching Authority. Along the way all may derive strength and comfort from prayerful and active union with the Two Hearts.

They constitute a school where we have to learn: how might is allied with meekness, power with humility, compassion with justice. Together the Two Hearts teach us how our salvation was wrought; together they listen to our prayer, especially the prayer of consecration and of reparation, the Mother adding her voice to ours, the Son desirous to show honour to his Mother, to manifest her true dignity.

Over all this partnership in efficacy and splendour lies mystery, the mystery of a shining all-powerful eternal design opening its way through the shadows, if not the darkness that shrouds so many lives.

There are three questions which she should briefly address: How does devotion to the Two Hearts help us to reflect profitably on the mysteries of the life of Christ? How is devotion to St. Joseph cultivated in harmony with an attitude towards the Alliance of the Two Hearts? Can we say broadly how Christian thought has dealt with the theme through the ages?

With regard to the first question, each one has to rely on the Gift of Piety. By this Gift the Holy Spirit guides each one along his or her strictly individual path. There is no mass production of holiness; there is total respect from the divine artist for every personal variable, problem, obstacle. Now in seeking to know and assimilate the mysteries of Christ, from the infancy, through the Hidden Life, in the Baptism, along the varied paths of the Public Life, in the Passion, death and Resurrection, always there is a certainty that the perfection in each instance exhibited, is the work of the Holy Spirit. He is the author of the masterpiece of perfection which Jesus Christ embodies; he is especially the artisan of the intimate bond between the Heart of Jesus and the Heart of Mary. She is never absent from him and it is in their two Hearts that they think, feel, and react together, within these two Hearts that they take to safety all of us for whom they lived and died.

(vi)

A problem seemed to arise in regard to St. Joseph. As one of the Holy Family should he not be included in the Alliance of the Hearts? St. Joseph himself is our best ally in the search for truth in this matter. All his perfection, the graces brought to him in his special predestination, depended intrinsically on his marriage with the

Blessed Virgin Mary. Now before that marriage, during Mary's betrothal, there occurred the vital moment for the alliance of the Hearts of Jesus and Mary. In the moment of the Annunciation Mary by her consent brought the Heart of Jesus into existence; by her acceptance of virginal motherhood she gave her flesh, and it was hers alone to bring him to reality. These two acts were unique, and St. Joseph would be the first to protest if we sought to attribute to him a role therein — as Our Lady would be the first to protest if we, in excessive eulogy of her perfection, were to proclaim her a goddess!

Is there then no place for St. Joseph in this heavenly, healing and ennobling partnership? Do we have to support the boycott of the great Son of David effected by the Second Vatican Council, to which allusion has been made? Do we ally ourselves with those who seek to marginalise this greatest Jew in the life of Christ, after him and his Blessed Mother? Do we have to erase from the charter documents of our Christian faith the vibrant, luminous passages in the Infancy Narratives of Luke and especially of Matthew which establish his status, clarify for all time his priority over all others after Jesus and Mary, record accurately his entire fidelity to his vocation?

The answer to these questions: Joseph is the first and perfect model of devotion to the two Hearts. That was his unique destiny. From him therein we have to learn. It would be tragic if we were to neglect the one who was for years the privileged intimate of Jesus, their hearts beating as one, the devoted spouse of Mary, first beneficiary of the generosity which comes from her Immaculate Heart. None can vie with Joseph here. If we honour those who, through the history of the Church, were favoured with apparitions of the Sacred Heart of Jesus or of the Immaculate Heart of Mary, these encounters lasting but for short periods of time, how shall we mark our esteem and gratitude towards the one who for years enjoyed the physical and spiritual presence of the Redeemer and Co-Redemptress, whose loving duty it was to provide friendship manifold to each, as legal and adoptive father, as true married spouse, breadwinner, guarantor of civic, Davidic status, in moments of danger secure protector. In view of such things it would be nigh impossible to foster and diffuse devotion to the Two Hearts without constant prayer to Joseph and trust in his intercessory power. All should be enclosed in a keen alert consciousness of the Jewish civilization of the heart, at the very centre of which, at its culminating point, bowing before the Hearts of Jesus and Mary, stands one, with them pre-eminent in the Poor of Yahweh, enriched with the flawless heritage of the Chosen People, Joseph, now patron of the universal Church, guardian of Christian families, patron of those who work as God's instruments to preserve the beauty of creation and to use the fruits of the earth to sustain the human race.[5]

Our third question is historical and is better treated in a separate chapter.

---

[5] On St. Joseph cf. articles, *Joseph, St.* pp. 206-209 and *Doubt, St. Joseph's*, p. 123f with extensive bibliographies, M.O'Carroll, *Theotokos*; for recent papal teaching, *Le Voci*, 19 March, 1961, Papal Letter, John XXIII proclaiming the saint protector of the Second Vatican Council and John Paul II, *Redemptoris Custos*, 15 August, 1989, Apostolic Exhortation; the Pope has in public addresses returned to the theme more than once; recent theological writing on the saint has sought a more meaningful title than foster-father, *Adoptive Father* preferably, and a review of exegesis of Mt. 1:18-21 in favour of St. Joseph's perception of an intervention by the Spirit — he awaited light on his role.

One would not expect from Vatican II such language as this from the Apostolic letter of John XXIII, Pope of the Council, the one therefore to whom it owed its existence, naming St. Joseph it Protector: "O, St. Joseph! here, here in your place as universal protector of the Church, we have wished to offer you through the voices and documents of our immediate predecessors of the last century — Pius IX to Pius XII — a garland of honours, the echoes of the testimonies of affectionate veneration, which rise now from all Catholic nations and from all missionary regions. Protect us always. May your interior spirit of peace, of silence, of good work and of prayer, in the service of the Holy Church, animates us always and encourages us in union with your blessed Spouse, our gentle and Immaculate Mother, in the strong and sweet love of Jesus, the glorious and immortal King of ages and of nations. Amen." In the Apostolic Letter which closed with these words, John XXIII recalled what every single Pope from Pius IX to his immediate predecessor, Pius XII, had done to honour St. Joseph. In each he saw the wish and action to promote enlightened devotion to the saint. He announced a special intention: "We intend, and make it our intention as of today, 19 March, 1961, that the altar of St. Joseph (in St. Peter's) shall acquire a new, greater and more solemn splendour, and that it shall become a point of attraction and of religious piety for individual souls and for great gatherings. Under the vaults of the Vatican church there will gather around the Head of the Church, the legions forming the Apostolic College, convened from all parts, even from the most distant points of the earth, for the Ecumenical Council." Thus spoke the Pope of the Council for a Council which refused to publish any teaching on the mighty saint. Is there a price to pay for such failure?

The Alliance of the Hearts of Jesus and Mary: Hope for the World

Chapter VI
Testimony of the Ages

(i)

The early centuries of church history saw sharp fundamental debates destined to clarify the essential truths of our faith, the Incarnation, the Holy Trinity, Mary's divine motherhood. Her closeness to her divine Son in his redemptive mission was caught in a most illuminating intuition found in very early, respected writings: she was the New Eve. Newman thought that this was the key to a whole understanding of her place in our religion. The great early thinkers also articulated the theory of her power to intervene in the life of the Church and of its members. Not only by example, but by action modeled on the mediation of her divine Son. Especially in the East she was styled Mediatress, and with time, in the East, in the West later, all the implications of this Pauline word were brought out.

We find authors speaking of her Heart. But it is with the first great saint of the Sacred Heart, St. Gertrude, that we get an intimation of Mary's Heart acting in parallel way to the Heart of her divine Son.

However, as Pope John Paul II said to the members of the Fatima symposium, it is in seventeenth century France that we find the most complete doctrinal, spiritual and liturgical response to the revelation of the Hearts of Jesus and Mary. Among the gifted writers of that age who occasionally touched on our theme, one is wholly conspicuous, St. John Eudes. We have met his name already in our reflection on the Immaculate Heart of Mary. Now he deserves greater attention, for he is abundant and utterly orthodox in regard to the two Hearts and he had been, very sadly, neglected.

The saint came under the influence of a luminary of the age, Pierre (later Cardinal) de Berulle, founder of the Oratory in France; Jean Eudes was a member. Eventually he founded two religious societies: Priests of Jesus and Mary, and a sisterhood, Our Lady of Charity of Refuge; a later branch of this was the Good Shepherd.

(ii)

In 1909, St. Pius X beatified John Eudes; in 1925, Pius XI canonised him. Both pontiffs in the respective Bulls of Beatification and of Canonization gave him the title of *Father, Doctor and Apostle of the Sacred Hearts of Jesus and Mary*. He is therefore the saint for our time. As we have seen, he celebrated the first feast in honour of the Heart of Mary, on 8 May, 1648. On 20 October, 1672, he celebrated the liturgical feast in honour of the Divine Heart of Jesus. His doctrinal outlook was evident in the letter he sent beforehand to his brothers in religion: "Our most lovable, kind Saviour has given our congregation a mysterious grace in the Admirable Heart of his Blessed Mother, the founder, the superior, the Heart of the life of this Congregation. He has been offering us this gift since the birth of this Congregation. Despite the fact that we have not until today, celebrated in a special feast the Adorable Heart of Jesus, we have never separated the two realities which God has united so intimately: the august Heart of the Son of God and that of his Blessed Mother."[1]

The saint insisted on the unity between Jesus and Mary: "I can only tell you that you must never separate what God has so perfectly united. So closely are Jesus and Mary bound up with each other that whoever has devotion to Jesus, has devotion to Mary. Jesus and Mary are the two first foundations of the Christian religion, the two living springs of all our blessings, the two centuries of all our devotion, and the two objectives you should keep in view in all your acts and works."[2]

St. John viewed the heart in three perspectives, as the bodily organ expressive of all that passes through the human being, as the sum of the interior life and as God himself acting in each one. He was accustomed to speak of the Heart of Jesus and Mary. He com-

---

[1] Apud A. Torres, *St. Jean Eudes*, p. 42 and Paul Milcent, CJM, *Saint John Eudes, Initiator of Christian Renewal in the 17th century,* tr. Br. John Connolly F.I.C., MS ed., p. 296f.; cf. Also *The Admirable Heart of Mary*, tr. C. di Targiani and Ruth Hauser, New York, 1948, pp. 24ff; occasional references to the Sacred Heart in *The Kingdom of Jesus*, New York, 1946; cf. following note.

[2] *The Kingdom of Jesus*, p. 271; cf. P. Milcent, D Sp, VIII, 488-501.

posed a Salutation to the Heart of Jesus and Mary, which is rather like a litany: for example: "Hail, Heart most holy; Hail, Heart most gentle; ... Hail most loving Heart of Jesus and Mary, we revere thee, we praise thee."

The saint did not avoid doctrinal explanations: "Although the Heart of Jesus is distinct from that of Mary," he writes, "and infinitely surpasses it in excellence and holiness, nevertheless, God has so closely united these two Hearts that we may say with truth that they are but one, because they have always been animated with the same spirit and filled with the same sentiments and affections. If St. Barnard could say he had but one heart with Jesus: '*Bene mihi est, cor unum cum Jesu habeo,*' and if it was said of the first Christians that they had but one heart and one soul, so great was the union amongst them, how much more can we say that Jesus and Mary had but one Heart and one soul, considering how closely they were bound together by the perfect conformity of mind, will and sentiment that existed between the divine Son of God and his Immaculate Mother. Add to this that Jesus so lives and reigns in Mary that he is the soul of her soul, the Spirit of her spirit, the Heart of her heart; so much so that we might well say that Jesus is enshrined in the Heart of Mary so completely that in honouring and glorifying her Heart, we honour and glorify Jesus Christ himself. O Jesus, living in the Heart of Mary! be the life of my heart. Mary, Mother of Jesus, obtain by thy intercession, I beseech thee, that I may have but one heart with thy beloved Son and thyself."[3]

St. John was inspired by this ideal which he expressed in language exuberant and graphic to make a unique contribution to French Catholicism in his time, as a preacher, as a spiritual guide, as a truly great religious founder: a spiritual giant of the ages.

(iii)

We move forward to the eighteenth century. In the domain of Marian doctrine and devotion in begins badly and gets progres-

---

[3] *Meditations on Various Subjects*, tr. Rev. Charles Lebrun, C.J.M., New York, 1947, p. 24f; cf. O. Schneider, *Der Prophet des Herzens Joannes Eudes*, Vienna, 1947.

sively worse; in the end we reach one of the lowest points in this particular history. But as ever, in bad spiritual situations there are moments, persons who bring partial relief. We may consider two in regard to the theme which here occupies us. One comes at the beginning of the eighteenth century, the other is at the end, and brings us into the nineteenth: Fr. Joseph de Gallifet, S.J. (1663-1749) and Fr. Pierre Joseph de Cloriviere, S.J. (1735-1822). They are not well known, which is very much to be regretted. Fr. de Gallifet was deeply involved with the promotion of the public cult of the Sacred Heart of Jesus. In this concerted effort a memorial submitted by the Polish hierarchy was decisive; it was, for one third of its content, borrowed from Fr. de Gallifet's book on the subject. What concerns us here is the section added to his book wherein he develops his theory on the Sacred Heart of Mary (his exact words). This is a substantial appendix and in it the author makes significant points on the relationship between the two Hearts.

The author recalls the growth of devotion to the Heart of Mary in the wake of devotion to the Sacred Heart of Jesus. He reminds us that Mary in the work of our Redemption by her union with her divine Son became "Mediatress and Mother." Coming to our essential problem he writes: "We may make the same reflections on the Heart of Mary that we have already made with regard to that of Jesus, and after the Heart of Jesus there never has been one so worthy of our admiration, our veneration and our love, as the Heart of Mary. We may then, with proper reservations, apply to this Sacred Heart all that we have said of the excellence of the Heart of Jesus....In fact, we may consider the Heart of Mary in two ways, as we have considered the Heart of Jesu: either in itself and with reference to its own excellence, or in regard to men."[4]

What follows is very enlightening on the Immaculate Heart. These words we may quote: "Let us approach the Eternal Father through the Heart of Jesus. Let us approach Jesus through the Heart of Mary. Through the Heart of Jesus let us pay to the Eternal Father what we owe his majesty, his justice, and his infinite mercy; and through the Heart of Mary, let us discharge what we owe to the

---

[4] *Le Coeur Adorable de Jesus*, Paris, Nouniol, 1861; English tr. 3rd ed., London, 1897, Part III, ch. 4, p. 241.

Son, in consideration of his greatness, his clemency, his bountiful goodness, his favours and his love. We shall obtain all from the Father through the Heart of the Mother."[5]

(iv)

Fr. de Cloriviere had to make his way through upheavals. First a storm struck the Society of Jesus; in 1773, Clement XIV pronounced it at an end. Fifteen years later it was the French Revolution, which hit him personally, as his nephew was involved in an assassination plot against Napoleon. From 1793 to 1809 he was either in hiding, or in prison, or under police surveillance. When the Revolution passed and Pius VII restored the Society of Jesus, de Cloriviere was given the task of reorganisation; he also busied himself with his religious foundations.

These concern us principally. In 1790, as the Revolution veered towards excess and militarism, Fr. de Cloriviere founded two societies, *Priests of the Heart of Mary* and *Daughters of the Heart of Mary*, the first religious institutes given this patronage. An innovator in the lifestyle he planned for his religious — these were the first sisters not bound to a religious habit, the zealous priest resisted the evils of the time, Marian to the core, he deplored the decline in devotion to Our Lady. His approach to her was directly to her Heart. At the age of 26, he had written: "May the Heart of her who is par excellence the Mother of Sorrows be our refuge also. Let us forget our afflictions to think of hers, and let us draw from this lovely Heart, source of fair love, the purest eagerness for him whom all should love."[6]

The founder saw the unity which we are dealing with: "After the three adorable Persons of the Holy Trinity, I must offer continual cult to the holy humanity of Christ and of his Blessed Mother. Jesus and Mary will always be present to my mind; I shall never cease to offer Jesus to the eternal Father and Mary to Jesus. In union with them I must pray, suffer and do all things. These two Sacred

---

[5] *Ibid.*, p. 258.

[6] H. Monier-Vinard, *Pierre de Cloriviere d'apres ses notes intimes*, I, Paris-Spes, 1935, p. 51.

Hearts will be my place of rest, my oratory, my school, my refuge, my centre. Nothing will be able to draw me from there. Each day my love, my reverence, and my trust in Jesus and in Mary must grow and I shall strive to inspire like sentiments in others."[7]

With these personal, intimate notes one may compare what de Cloriviere wrote in a letter included in the Circulars sent to his newly founded sisterhood. "I have said that the Heart of Jesus is entirely in the Heart of Mary. I am surprised that an expression so simple, based on the language of Scripture could have shocked you. You do not know in the heart it is often the soul that is understood, it is the person relatively to acts of the will. Nothing more acceptable in ordinary language, nothing more common in sacred language. Almost all the texts where the heart is mentioned, even if taken at random, have this meaning." De Cloriviere then quotes Gen 6:6; Mt 22:37; Rom 5:5.[8]

The Heart of Mary is seen in the total mystery of her unique calling. Thus, when de Cloriviere was challenged on the statement that "the Heart of Mary has as gift what the Heart of Jesus has of himself," he replies: "Doubtless, when you rebuked me over this statement, when it appeared exaggerated to you, you had but superficially studied it. The words 'as gift' express all the reservations desirable. They assert that Mary has nothing of herself, is nothing of herself, is a pure creature, that there is an infinite distance between God and her, between her Son and her, that she possessed nothing which she has not received, which the infinite Wisdom of God thought fitting to give her in the actual order of Providence." He related all God's gifts to her divine motherhood.

The reservation so well phrased served de Cloriviere also to counter another critique made of his doctrine — he had said that "the Heart of Mary bears all the features of the Heart of Jesus, it comes as close to the Heart of the man-God as could the heart of a pure creature." In addition, de Cloriviere invoked the Eve-Mary typology with his explanation of this truth: "Eve, both in her body and soul, was in all things like to Adam, as far as was compatible with the diversity of the sexes. In the spiritual sense, that must be

---

[7] Apud A. Rayez, S.J. in Maria, ed. H. du Manoir, S.J., III, p. 316.
[8] *Lettres circulaires of Fr. de Cloriviere*, Paris, Durassie, 389-390.

understood much more perfectly of Jesus and Mary. Remark, too, that consideration of the heart is essential in the parallel with Jesus Christ from the viewpoint of his humanity."[9]

The life and teaching of this remarkable spiritual writer raise questions. One is in regard to his sources. He does not seem directly dependent on St. John Eudes, though the latter's influence may have reached him through Fr. de Gallilfet. It is also intriguing to ponder why his intuition and the work which embodied it did not have a wider impact in the life of the Church. De Cloriviere's ideas were a powerful challenge to the rationalism of the Enlightenment, as to the power and violence which accompanied the Revolution. We cannot measure the effect of spiritual phenomena, personal or collective, in the flow of the supernatural through time.

When we come to the early nineteenth century, there seems little to report doctrinally in regard to the two Hearts. In the first years Fr. de Condrin founded the missionaries of Picpus, named for the Hearts of Jesus and Mary. With little time to compose a formal treatise, he did express his ideal in his correspondence: for example: "If in truth one is deeply touched by the tenderness of the Heart of Jesus for the salvation of souls, how can one not be inflamed with zeal to answer the love of such a kind Master? If one thinks often of the motherly tenderness of the Heart of Mary for men who have become her children in the person of St. John, how could one not feel one's soul on fire with a holy zeal to honour the Virgin of virgins?"

(v)

Yet we can quote two theologians of the greatest stature from the nineteenth century. In each case it is a brief word in a vast corpus, but let the reader judge its significance. M.J. Scheeben writes thus: "In recent years the devotion to Christ's sacred humanity is concentrated in the devotion to his Sacred Heart, and is thus deepened, vivified and as it were, transformed....In an analogous way, with ecclesiastical permission and approval, the devotion to the most pure Heart of Mary has been developed. Both devotions have a

---

[9] *Ibid.*

profound theological foundation. Their special object forms, as it were, the focus to which is brought the entire fullness and greatness of Catholic thought regarding Christ's human nature and Mary's person. From this focal point the thought can be clearly elucidated on all sides. In the case of Christ, the heart can be regarded only as member of his body, and thus formally represents only his human nature. In the case of Mary, the heart is the life-centre of her person and, as such, it represents the latter even in the maternal, distinguishing mark of her person, since the heart is the instrument of her physical and spiritual motherhood. The profound and dogmatic grounds defining the devotion to Jesus' Sacred Heart and to the most pure Heart of Mary present both Hearts in an intimate and organic union. They justify also the union of both as objects of devotion, and, therefore, their being represented side by side."[10]

Thus Scheeben is sometimes spoken of as the greatest theologian of the nineteenth century. Not all would accept the bare statement that Christ's Heart can be regarded "only as member of his body." Like all in his human nature, it is hypostatically united to the Word and is adorable. In general intellectual influence, Scheeben is possibly surpassed by Newman, who will, one day, if the prediction of Pius XII is fulfilled, be not only canonised, but proclaimed a Doctor of the Church. Mention has been made of his devotion to the Immaculate Heart of Mary, expressed in a beautiful Litany, replete with doctrine. He saw the importance of devotion to the Sacred Heart. Let us quote the final antiphon and response to the Litany and the concluding prayer: "Immaculate Mary, meek and humble of heart: conform our hearts to the Heart of Jesus." "O most merciful God, who for the salvation of sinners and the refuge of the wretched, hast made the Immaculate Heart of Mary most like in tenderness and pity to the Heart of Jesus, grant that we, who now commemorate her most sweet and loving heart, may by her merits and intercession, ever live in the fellowship of the Hearts of both Mother and Son, through the same Christ our Lord."[11]

---

[10] M.J. Scheeben, *Mariology*, St. Louis, vol. II, 1955, tr. T.L.M.J. Geukers, p. 273; there too Scheeben deals with the problem of St. Joseph, as it has been already answered in the present book.

[11] J.H. (Cardinal) Newman, *Meditations and Devotions*, London, 1894, pp. 333-336.

(vi)

To conclude these testimonies, which have some repetition of what has been stated already, I shall reproduce the exact words which the children at Fatima claimed that they heard from the Angel of Peace during three apparitions in the course of the year 1916:

1. "Pray thus (following his instructions). The Hearts of Jesus and Mary are attentive to the voice of your supplications."

2. "Pray, pray very much! The most holy Hearts of Jesus and Mary have designs of mercy on you. Offer prayers and sacrifices constantly to the Most High."

3. "Most holy Trinity, Father, Son, and Holy Spirit, I offer you the most precious Body, Blood, Soul and Divinity of Jesus Christ, present in all the tabernacles in reparation for the outrages, sacrileges and indifferences with which he himself is offended. And through the infinite merits of his Most Sacred Heart, and the Immaculate Heart of Mary, I beg of you the conversion of poor sinners."[12]

In this year was manifest to the children, the favoured witnesses of the events and messages of 1917, the origin of the whole drama of power, love and mercy, which has continued until now and does not decline. It was the Alliance of the Two Hearts.

(vii)

As we approach the day of Christian unity, it is important to consider similarities as well as differences between eastern and western spirituality and devotion. John Paul II, influenced here to our enlightenment by his expertise in phenomenology, as by biblical reflection, and especially by his recent profound study of Orthodox theology, provides a valuable introduction to the subject:

"A certain trend in humanistic culture has led many men and women of our time to turn away from God. But with the decline of the great ideologies, it has become dramatically clear that when man becomes 'bereft of God,' he loses the meaning of his own life and in some way becomes 'bereft' of himself. Who is man? Chris-

---

[12] *Fatima in Lucia's own words*, introduction, notes by Fr. J.M. Alonso, C.M.F., 1976, pp. 62,63; cf. Fr. Alonso in *Ephemerides Mariologicae*, 22(1972), pp. 241,242.

tianity, in its twofold tradition of East and West, has always taken this question seriously. It has given rise to a profound, harmonious anthropology based on the principle that the ultimate truth of the human being is to be sought in the One who created him.

"Eastern spirituality makes a specific contribution to authentic knowledge of man by insisting on the perspective of the heart. Christians of the East love to distinguish three types of knowledge. The first is limited to man in his bio-psychic structure. The second remains in the realm of moral life. The highest degree of self-knowledge is obtained, however, in contemplation, by which man returns deeply into himself, recognizes himself as the divine image and, purifying himself of sin, meets the living God to the point of becoming 'divine' himself by the gift of grace.

"This is knowledge of the heart. Here the 'heart' means much more than a human faculty, such as affectivity, for example. It is rather the principle of personal unity, a sort of 'interior space' in which the person recollects his whole self so as to live in the knowledge and love of the Lord. Eastern authors are referring to this principle that was placed in it in view of his coming: 'God spoke of old to our fathers at various times and in many ways by means of the prophets. But he has at the end of these days spoken to us in his Son, whom he has appointed heir of all things, and through whom he made the world'(Heb 1:1-2)."[13]

Can we then see in the wondrous central truth of Old Testament anthropology, the heart of man speaking to God, the basis of a high synthesis of Orthodox and Catholic spirituality, the "attention to the heart" of the Orthodox, the Sacred Heart revealed to Catholics, calling poignantlly for the total attention which is his right. Jesus the Jew, God incarnate, drawing from the depthless divine treasure of his people that which will give full meaning to the words he spoke to Gertrude, Margaret Mary, and those presently of their lineage.

Catholics like the present writer, who believe in the absolute primacy of Christ, see it taught in Col 1:16-17: "For through him

---

[13] ORE 1996, no. 40(1460), 2 October, text of Angelus address 29 September, 1996. On the "attention to the heart" in Orthodox spirituality cf. T. Spiklik, D Sp XI, 996f.

all things were created in heaven and on earth, the visible and the invisible, whether thrones or lordships or rulers or authorities; they were all created through him and for him, and he is himself before all, and in him all things hold together." Christ was not an afterthought of the Father consequent on the sin of Adam; because of the sin he came as a Redeemer who was from all eternity foreseen as the One for whom creation would exist. Thus he will be seen in the final consummation; then his Heart will be the very focus of the entire universe, the inexhaustible source of power and splendour.

The Alliance of the Hearts of Jesus and Mary: Hope for the World

Chapter VII
John Paul II

I – Letter to Cardinal Sin, President of the International Symposium on the Alliance of the Hearts of Jesus and Mary

I am pleased to offer my cordial greetings to all the participants in the International Symposium on the Alliance of the Hearts of Jesus and Mary taking place in Fatima on 14-19 September, 1986. As you begin your proceedings, I wish to assure you of my spiritual closeness and of my encouragement for the fruitful outcome of your exchange.

Your symposium will provide biblical scholars and theologians the valuable opportunity for reflecting on devotion to the Sacred Heart of Jesus and the Immaculate Heart of Mary in the perspective of Sacred Scripture and Tradition. Much research has already been done on devotion to the Sacred Heart of Jesus, but it is your aim to focus attention on the Immaculate Heart of Mary and the interrelation of love between the hearts of the Son of God and of his Mother. Your reflection will also endeavor to explain the Christian's participation in these mysteries and thereby render a worthwhile service to the whole Church by clarifying the importance of devotion to the Hearts of Jesus and Mary.

We can say that just as the mystery of Redemption began in the womb of the Virgin Mary, so did that splendid union of the Hearts of Christ and his Mother. From the very moment when the Word was made flesh beneath the Heart of Mary, there has existed under the influence of the Holy Spirit an enduring relationship of love between them. The Heart of the Mother has always followed the redemptive mission of her Son. As Jesus hung on the Cross in completion of his salvific work, Simeon's prophecy foretelling the definitive alliance of the Hearts of the Son and of the Mother was fulfilled: "And a sword will pierce your own soul too" (Lk 2:35). Indeed the centurion's lance that pierced the side of Christ penetrated the Heart of his sorrowful Mother, and sealed it in sacrificial love.

Since the Hearts of Jesus and Mary are joined forever in love, we know that to be loved by the Son is also to be loved by his Mother. At the foot of the Cross, Mary was proclaimed our Mother, and her Immaculate Heart now continues to enfold us with the same maternal love with which she loved her Son.

It is my prayer that your initiative will make the Alliance of the Hearts of Jesus and Mary better understood and appreciated by the People of God and thus promote devotion to the Hearts of the Son and His Mother in our own day. In the love of Christ and his Mother who pondered his mystery in her Heart (cf. Lk 2:51), I impart to you and all assembled at Fatima my Apostolic Blessing.

From the Vatican, 8 September, 1986.

Joannes Paulus II.

II – Address by Pope John Paul II to participants in the Fatima Symposium: The Vatican, 22 September, 1986

Dear Friends in Christ,

1. I am pleased to welcome all of you who have taken part in the International Symposium on the Alliance of the Hearts of Jesus and Mary that was held this past week in Fatima. I wish to greet in a special way Cardinal Sin, the President of your Symposium, and together with him, all who were responsible for formulating and carrying out the specific plans for your week of theological study. The title of your Symposium was taken from my Angelus address of 15 September, 1985, when I made reference to that "admirable alliance of Hearts of the Son of God and of his Mother." We can indeed say that devotion to the Sacred Heart of Jesus and to the Immaculate Heart of Mary has been an important part of the "*sensus fidei*" of the People of God during recent centuries. These devotions seek to direct our attention to Christ and to the role of his Mother in the mystery of Redemption, and, though distinct, they are inter-related by reason of the enduring relation of love that exists between the Son and the Mother.

2. Much research has been done on devotion to the Sacred Heart of Jesus. Hence you have made it your specific aim to reflect

upon devotion to the Immaculate Heart of Mary in the perspective of Sacred Scripture and Tradition, while at the same time concentrating on the intimate link that unites the Hearts of Jesus and his Mother. Devotion to the Heart of Mary cannot be traced to the early centuries of Christian history, though the Heart of Mary is indeed mentioned in the Gospel of Luke. There are some references to the Heart of the Mother of God in the commentaries upon the Scriptures by the Fathers of the Church, but for the most part it was not until the seventeenth century that under the influence of Saint John Eudes this devotion became widespread. In our own century we see that the message of Our Lady of Fatima, the consecration of the world in 1942 to the Immaculate Heart of Mary by my predecessor Pope Pius XII, and theological initiatives such as your own, have helped us to appreciate the importance of this devotion.

It is worthy of note that the Decree by which Pope Pius XII instituted for the universal Church the celebration in honour of the Immaculate Heart of Mary states: "With this devotion, the Church renders the honour due to the Immaculate Heart of the Blessed Virgin Mary, since under the symbol of this Heart she venerates with reverence the eminent and singular holiness of the Mother of God, and especially her most ardent love of God and Jesus her Son, moreover, her maternal compassion for all those redeemed by the divine Blood" (S.R.C., 4 Mary 1944; AAS 37, 1945, p. 50). Thus it can be said that our devotion to Mary's Immaculate Heart expresses our reverence for her maternal compassion both for Jesus and for all of us her spiritual children, as she stood at the foot of the Cross.

I presented this same thought in my first Encyclical, *Redemptor Hominis*, in which I pointed out that from the first moment of the Redemptive Incarnation, 'under the special influence of the Holy Spirit, Mary's Heart, the Heart of both a virgin and a mother, has always followed the work of her Son, and has gone out to all those whom Christ has embraced, and continues to embrace with inexhaustible love" (No. 22).

3. We see symbolized in the Heart of Mary her maternal love, her singular sanctity and her central role in the redemptive mis-

sion of her Son. It is with regard to her special role in her Son's mission that devotion to Mary's Heart has prime importance, for through love of her Son and of all humanity she exercises a unique instrumentality in bringing us to him.

The act of entrusting to the Immaculate Heart of Mary that I solemnly performed at Fatima on 13 May, 1982, and once again on 25 March, 1984, at the conclusion of the Extraordinary Holy Year of the Redemption, is based upon this truth of Mary's maternal love and particular intercessory role. If we turn to Mary's Immaculate Heart, she will surely "help us to conquer the menace of evil, which so easily takes roots in the hearts of the people of today, and whose immeasurable effects weigh down upon our modern world and seem to block the paths towards the future" (No. 3).

Our act of consecration refers ultimately to the Heart of her Son, for as the Mother of Christ, she is wholly united to his redemptive mission. As at the marriage feast of Cana, when she said, "Do whatever he tells you," Mary directs all things to her Son, who answers our prayers and forgives our sins. Thus by dedicating ourselves to the Heart of Mary, we discover a sure way to the Sacred Heart of Jesus, symbol of the merciful love of our Savior.

The act of entrusting ourselves to the Heart of Our Lady establishes a relationship of love with her in which we dedicate to her all that we have and are. This consecration is practised essentially by a life of grace, of purity, of prayer, of penance that is joined to the fulfillment of the duties of a Christian, and of reparation for our sins and the sins of the world.

My esteemed friends, I encourage you to continue your scholarly efforts to promote among the People of God a better understanding of devotion to the Hearts of the Son and of his Mother. I thank you for your presence here, and I assure you of my prayers for your worthy endeavors. In the love of the Hearts of Jesus and Mary, I impart to all of you my Apostolic Blessing.

I – Consensus Document of the 1986 Fatima Symposium on the Alliance of The Hearts of Jesus and Mary

These conclusions are the fruit of common search and fraternal discussions, and were accepted by all.

They were then submitted to the Holy Father, Pope John Paul II, by the participating theologians, through the hands of His Eminence Jaime Cardinal Sin, who was the Chairman of the symposium at Fatima.

The Holy Father, at the end of the symposium, received Cardinal Sin and the participants of the symposium, in Rome, on 22 September, 1986.

The Hearts of Jesus and Mary in Christian Piety

1.1 In modern Catholic piety, the devotion towards the Hearts of Jesus and Mary has been very widely spread throughout the world. This was preceded by a long historical process, a history which is richer than has often been realized (e.g. in Ekbert of Schoenau, in the school of Helfta, etc.). This widespread devotion is not to be found only in popular religiosity, but is also expressed in the Church's own liturgy - in the respective feasts which the Roman Pontiffs have decreed as feasts to be celebrated in the universal Church. In each case, the occasions which gave rise to this rapid growth of the devotion were charismatic phenomena: the apparitions at Paray-le-Monial (for the Heart of Jesus) and at Fatima (for the Heart of Mary). But these events were not the only "ground" for these devotions, but concrete texts for the Heart of Jesus: Mt 11:19; Jn 7:37ff; 19:33-37; for the Heart of Mary: Lk 2:19,51 and Lk 2:35.

1.2 When we turn our attention to the Hearts of Jesus and Mary, we do so in line with a basic datum in the Scriptures. In the Gospels there is an implicit anthropology, and this anthropology can rightly be described as "Christian." This anthropology underlines the preaching of Jesus (especially his controversies with the scribes). What is the true nucleus of this anthropology? It can be expressed in this fundamental thesis: "the heart" is the definitive element in man; the value of a human person is measured, we might say, by the "heart." St. Jerome understood this when he said: *"When it is* *asked where the seat of the soul is, Plato replies, 'In the brain.' But Jesus shows us that it is in the heart."*

1.3 Thus devotion toward Jesus, he who came in the flesh (1 Jn 4:2; 2 Jn 7) — a devotion which cannot prescind from his humanity, and our devotion too toward Mary, a human person of our own stock — such devotion must truly reach their "hearts." (Otherwise we would have a rather superficial devotion). In this sense, the *cultus* towards the Hearts of Jesus and Mary is not something optional, at the margins of our Catholic faith, but the very nucleus of that faith, in the sense that this *cultus* is directed toward Jesus and Mary, toward what is the principal reality of Jesus and Mary, *their Hearts.*

2.1 (What is "the heart"?). In the Christian anthropology we have referred to, "the heart" designates *the spiritual interiority of the human person*, that interiority which directs the entire life of the spirit and all its manifestations. "The heart" is the *hegemonikon* (the GHQ) in the human organ. For a fact, the word "heart" is the name of the concrete bodily organ. And it is certain that for a long time, it was held that the life of the soul had its seat in the physical, bodily heart. That this is not so, we have known for a long time. And yet, in man who has a bodily heart, the use of the word "heart" in a *spiritual sense* does have a real foundation, because the physical heart does in fact "feel" the intense repercussions of the psychological and spiritual states of the person. This is why, despite our knowledge that the soul of man does not "reside" in his physical heart, still the "heart" has remained as the symbol of the life of the spirit of man, the symbol especially of love. How wrong then are the people who say that the symbol of the human heart says nothing to modern man. Perhaps never has this symbol been so prevalent in its use in "secular life" as it is today. Furthermore, people do not consider as *merely* metaphorical the expressions they use when they use "heart" in a spiritual sense (e.g. "I love you with all my heart"; "I'm truly sorry, with all my heart" and the like). When someone says something like this, usually he experiences something real in his own physical heart.

2.2 Again the word "heart" (in its spiritual sense) refers to human interiority which, in some true way, is seen as something permanent, abiding. In our usual ways of talking, we do not say about a man who has done one single act, good or bad, that he has a good heart or a bad heart. When we say that: "He has a good heart" or "He has a bad heart," we are speaking of what is permanent, abiding in this man.

3.1 Given all this, we understand why the modern devotion towards the Hearts of Jesus and Mary began to take shape from consideration of "the inner states" of Jesus and Mary (Berulle). (True, this devotion later began to grow and spread in a striking way in the wake of charismatic events which were very important in the life of the Church). But the beginnings of this devotion in our times began with the consideration, not of the transitory actions of Jesus and Mary, but with their *interior states of spirit*. This kind of devotion was extended in the veneration of the inner life of Mary (Olier). Then these permanent *interior realities* began to be designated by the word "heart" — still understood as linked up with the physical heart (St. John Eudes).

3.2 This spiritual tradition teaches us the importance of turning to and considering the abiding love of Jesus and Mary toward each other, and the importance of the veneration of the richness of their interior life. This love, turned toward God and turned toward us, draws us powerfully, and invites us to place our hope in the Hearts of Jesus and Mary, and to call on them, to invoke them. When we use the word "heart" to designate these spiritual realities, we are really merely returning to that primitive Christian anthropology we have referred to. When we speak of "the Hearts" of Jesus and Mary, we also refer (in some way) to their physical Hearts, because we see the life of their souls as linked up with the physical Hearts.

3.3 When we consider the scenes in the Gospels, we cannot find their meaning unless we consider the love of Jesus (or the love of Mary) going forth from the Heart. That is going forth from the most intimate core of their life of the spirit, which makes that love intelligible to us. When we refer to Jesus, the love of God becomes present to us in his Heart (because it is the human Heart of a divine Person). With regard to the saving work achieved by Jesus, we know that the multiple events of his life are bound up together by that self-offering which Jesus made upon entering our world (cf. Heb 10:5ff) — that self-offering which stayed alive within his spirit all his life long, to his death on the Cross, that self-offering which lives on, through the ages, in his self-offering in heaven (cf. the homily of Pope John Paul II, at the Mass celebrated in Barcelona, 7 November, 1982).

3.4 Mary, as the new Eve, cooperated in this saving work of Christ. Her cooperation began with her consent to the Annunciation. It was sustained all her life long, especially when she stood at the foot of the Cross. It perdures unceasingly in heaven, through her intercession(cf. *Lumen Gentium*, 62).

The oblation of Jesus the Incarnate word, and the cooperation of Mary, are seen by us as realized in their "Hearts" (understood in the spiritual sense). We venerate this oblation and this cooperation as interior and abiding dispositions (and thus as even now actual), as dispositions of spirit, which are filled with love. And since we receive their love, the love of their Hearts, we are bound to love them in return.

4.1 Grateful love tends to imitation. Jesus invites us to imitate him, not by copying his external deeds, but by the effort to make the inner and abiding dispositions of his Heart ours, in imitating his very Heart (cf. Mt 11:29).

The Heart of Jesus was ever open to the needy, the poor and the suffering. He called the poor blessed (Lk 6:20). He pointed to the proclamation of the Gospel to the poor as the sign of the messianic presence in his own Person (cf. Lk 7:22). Jesus believed that he was sent to preach the Gospel to the poor, to heal those who were contrite in spirit, to proclaim the freeing of captives and the giving of sight to the blind, to set the downtrodden free, and to preach the year of the Lord's favour (cf. Lk 4:18ff).

His new commandment was that we should love one another as he himself has loved us (Jn 13:34; 15:17). It is by fulfilling this commandment that his disciples will become known (Jn 13:35). To imitate the Heart of Jesus (which follows on the devotion toward his Heart) does not bring on "alienation." No, rather, it impels us to make our own the preferential (but not exclusive) love for all the little ones, the despised ones, in the world.

4.2 Mary, for her part, she who always looked upon herself as a lowly maidservant of the Lord (cf. Lk 1:38-48), had the same sentiments with regard to the signs which accompany the coming of the messianic kingdom; the proud are humbled, the powerful are brought low, the lowly ones are exalted, the hungry are given their fill, the thirst of the parched is slaked (cf. Lk 2:51ff) — these signs show us the new order of things, in which justice — so long unfulfilled — at last reigns. Thus the Christian faithful experience the motherly presence of Mary in all the events of their own lives, whether in joy or sorrow. We imitate the intimate sentiments of Mary's Heart in the same way that we imitate those of Jesus.

5.1 The second Vatican Council has urged us to foster in ourselves intimate relationships with the saints who now reign with Christ (cf. LG 50). The Sacred Congregation for the Doctrine of the Faith has recently reaffirmed (17 May, 1979, AAS 17/1979, pp. 939-943), the theological teaching of the Church in matters of eschatology (keeping the entire teaching of the Tradition in view). We are taught that the subjects, in glory, of such relationships of friendship are the souls of the saints; these souls cry out before the Altar (cf. Apoc. 6:9ff). But Jesus and Mary, both of whom are risen, intercede for us in their total human existential reality. When we call on the Hearts of Jesus and Mary, we do not consider them as belonging to the past, but as living now; for the heavenly life, (the soul-life) of Jesus and of Mary is reflected even now, in their bodies and in their very Hearts. When we consider the Hearts of Jesus and Mary, our intimate relationships with them regards their entire human and glorious humanity, which they now possess in union of spirit and risen body. The just, those who are of Christ, will have their bodies with them in glory too, when the Parousia of the Lord takes place (cf. 1 Cor 15:23). For, to cite Tertullian (*De resurrectione carnis*, 34), how unworthy of God it would be, to save only half of man.

5.2 This leads us to understand why the Church encourages devotion toward the Hearts of Jesus and Mary, and not toward the hearts of the other saints. When it is a matter of the hearts of these other saints, we think of these hearts as having once lived and beat, and as living and beating again in glory in the future resurrection. (Sometimes, some of these hearts are preserved incorrupt, but then we venerate them as mere relics of the dead). In this sense our relations with the saints are never quite the same as our relations with Jesus and Mary. We place our hope in their living Hearts. We call only upon *their* Hearts, as living Hearts.

5.3 The complete human reality of our Lord is substantially present and, in an abiding way, in the Eucharist, which is the true body "which was born of the Virgin, which was offered up for the salvation of the world, which hung on the Cross, and now sits at the right hand of the Father," and which is the true blood "which poured out from his pierced side" (The oath of Berengar, DS 700)— For this reason the tabernacle is the privileged place for our intimate relationship with the inner life of Jesus — that inner life which we call "the heart" and with the existential human reality of Jesus. The whole of Eucharistic worship, sacramental participation in the sacrifice and in communion — is the very height of this intimacy.

II – The Alliance of the Two Hearts: The Heart of Jesus and the Heart of Mary

1.1 The devotion toward "the states," the interior life, the "Heart" — of both Jesus and Mary — began at the same time; this is quite certain (we find it e.g. already in Berulle). In a true sense, this devotion was developed first with regard to Mary, rather than with regard to Jesus. We see this in the personal development in the spirituality of St. John Eudes, who "found" the Heart of Jesus in the Heart of Mary.

1.2 One can readily understand this "joining together" of the two Hearts in spirituality and devotion. When one considers in a complete way the mystery of salvation, one cannot forget that the last Adam (cf. 1 Cor 15:45) has the new Eve with him, the new Eve who has cooperated in the work of salvation (cf. the parallelism between the first Eve and Mary, in Justin's *Dialogue with Trypho,* 100). This is a very ancient tradition, and it alludes to the nuptial image, to bring to light the alliance which exists between Jesus and Mary.

1.3 This alliance or covenant began at the calling of Mary in the Annunciation. This calling (this vocation) finds in Mary the virginal Heart (Lk 1:34) — a Heart thus ready, under the guidance of the Holy Spirit, to give itself freely and fully, in undivided response to God's call. Thus was the linking up of the Hearts of the Mother and the Son begun, a linking up which would remain valid forever.

1.4 In the opening prayer (the "Collect") of the text of the first Mass written by St. John Eudes for the Heart of the Mary, this joining of the Heart of the Son and the Heart of the Mother is very forcefully affirmed and extolled. Because the work of Christ proceeds from his "Heart," and the cooperation of Mary proceeds from hers, then devotion to the great mystery of our faith (*magnum pietatis mysterium*, cf. 1 Tim 3:16) would be wholly incomplete without the consideration of these two Hearts.

2.1 The covenant/alliance between the Hearts of Jesus and Mary must be seen "within" the theology of the New Alliance set up for the messianic age, as foretold by *the prophets*. There is express mention of this in Jer 31:33. There is clear allusion to it in Ex 36:28 when God promises that he will gather a new people: "And you shall be my own people, and I shall be your God." The newness of this people will consist in the gift given to it of a *new heart*. The old heart of stone will be replaced by a new heart of flesh (Ez. 36:26). The law of God will not be any longer just a dead law, from outside, but a new law, written in the heart of the new people (cf. Jer 31:33).

2.2 Mary, *as Daughter of Sion*, is the beginning of this new people of God. By a wonderful act of the Spirit, the Heart of Mary, from her first moment of existence, is already prepared (*The Immaculate Conception*).

All her life long, Mary is led by the Holy Spirit, so that she might cooperate, in all readiness and obedience, with the grace of God.

At the moment of the Annunciation, she gave her total consent to her vocation (Lk 1:38). Thus she joined her fate indissolubly with the life and destiny of her Son. Thus did she seal a covenant, an alliance with her Son, as she was bidden to, by the message of the angel.

At the *foot of the Cross*, in her own Heart, she became the sharer of the sorrows of her Son, who was there giving his life for us. In that hour, when the sword of sorrow transfixed her soul, or her Heart (cf. Lk 2:35, "thy own Heart a sword shall pierce"), Jesus revealed the spiritual motherhood of the Virgin of her Son Jesus, so that he might be the first-born among many brothers (Rom 8:29). Mary fulfills this mission given to her, because she had participated — as his Mother, Mother of the Saviour — in the passion of her Son, now as Mother of the Son of God, she constantly intercedes that the new people of the new covenant may be gathered together (*Pentecost*).

This ecclesiological dimension of the mission of Mary is very clearly extolled in the liturgical texts approved by Pope Pius XII (and revised by Pope Paul VI). It is clear that already in the Cana-event, we see Mary inviting all of us to enter into the new covenant also, by doing whatever Jesus bids us to do (cf. Jn 2:5).

2.3 After Jesus, from the Cross, proclaimed that his disciples should look upon Mary as their own mother (Jn 19:27), no one can henceforth be the disciple of Jesus without taking Mary into his own keeping (*eis to idia*). Thus Pope Paul VI could say, "If we wish to be Christian, we must be Marian" (Paul VI at the shrine of Bonaria, 24 April, 1970). Thus the bond between Mary and Jesus, which is present in the depths of their Hearts, is made manifest once again. And this bond is expressed in the liturgy, since both in Rome (from 1880) and in the universal Church (from the time of the liturgical reform of Pope Paul VI), the celebration of the feast of the Heart of Mary is immediately joined with the feast of the Sacred Heart of Jesus.

2.4 The covenant/alliance between the Hearts of Jesus and Mary tends towards the formation of the new people of God, no longer with the heart of stone within them, but the heart of flesh. If this is so, then it is clear that no people would truly be God's true people, unless all of us who belong to this new people of God, undertake the effort to build up just social structures. To live "without affection" and "without mercy" (Rom 1:31) is not the way of Christians, but rather the way of those "who imprison the truth of God in injustice" (Rom 1:18).

3.1 The opening of the Heart of Christ by the lance of the soldier (cf. Jn 19:34) should set in motion the fulfillment of the prophet Zechariah's prophecy: "They shall look upon him whom they have pierced" (Jn 19:37 and Zech 12:10). If we read what follows in Zechariah, we shall see that the text speaks of the mourning of one who mourns for his only son. We are sinners, and thus we pierce the Heart of Jesus; therefore, we must go back to that Heart with *sorrow for our sins*. The first act of *reparation* toward the Heart of Christ is our own *conversion*. And moved by the love of our brethren, sincerely we must grieve too for those who make no reparation for their own sins, and in our sorrow for them we also intercede their conversion. Jesus has given us the commandment to love our enemies (cf. Mt 5:44). Thus our *reparation for others* admits of no limits. Rather, without excepting anyone, we entrust all to the mercy of God.

3.2 Because Mary shared in the passion of her Son through the pain in her own Heart, our sins too were the cause of her motherly compassion. Our sins were also the reason for her compassion in our regard. Thus our sentiments and deeds of **reparation** should reach out to Mary too, for her Heart is intimately linked with the Heart of Christ himself.

III – Consecration to the Hearts of Jesus and Mary and "The Alliance of the Two Hearts"

1. Every Christian is fundamentally and primarily consecrated in baptism. Through baptism the Christian is consecrated to the Holy Trinity. The mission of Jesus, "to baptize them in the name" (Mt 28:19) means this: "to baptize them in the service of the Father, the Son and the Spirit."

2.1 If we analyze what the baptism of an adult person involves, we will see that the first initiative comes from God, who, by his grace, calls the human person to faith and conversion. In the second moment, this person responds to this call and vocation, by coming to baptism freely and in faith. In the act of baptism itself, *it is God who* **consecrates** the person being baptized. As St. Augustine says, "It is Christ himself who baptizes" (Tract. in Joannis Evang., 6,7). Christ makes the baptized person holy. The baptized person is *consecrated* ("theologically passive"; the *agent* there is *God*). This baptismal consecration, in one way or another, is renewed in every sacrament.

2.2 Every baptized person is bound to live in a way that is in keeping with the character of a "holy person," that is, as one consecrated to the service of the Holy Trinity. This implies not only the effort to live a personal life of holiness, but also the generous striving to give evangelical witness in the world. The Christian who lives a life of holiness is truly a witness to Christ; this witnessing life will of course include a confession of faith explicitly (in word). It is for this that he/she has been consecrated in baptism; for this that Confirmation comes with further strength and energy; for this that the Eucharist is received as food and nourishment. These three steps in Christian initiation all lead to the same objective. Every other gift of the Spirit invites him/her to move forward, with fidelity, toward the same purpose. Thus every Christian is not only called to his/her conversion, but he/she must be a servant of the consecration of others, of all peoples, and the servant of their oneness in the Holy Spirit.

2.3 The spiritual tradition of the Church, however, also recognizes *other "consecrations"* which come after baptism. These are acts by which the Christian commits himself/herself, in one way or another, to lead a more stable way of life which will enable him/her to fulfill more readily the consecration of Baptism, and to live that consecration in all its consequences. Thus, all other post-baptismal consecrations have no other purpose than the baptismal consecration itself. In these other consecrations there must be found both the desire and will for personal holiness and authentic apostolic intent.

2.4 The way we speak of these post-baptismal consecrations shows the profound difference between them and the consecration which God himself makes of the baptized person in Baptism. When we speak of post-baptismal consecrations, we say the *person consecrated himself/herself* (in the reflexive mode, rather than in the "theologically passive" mode).

2.5 We must point out that a person makes these acts of consecration under the influence of grace which impels him/her to an ever fuller gift of self. On the other hand, the Christian who thus consecrates himself/herself to God, asks God to receive his/her oblation, and to give the grace necessary for living out this consecration in life itself.

3. The same spiritual tradition of the Church also recognizes consecration to Mary. Let us not wonder (or be surprised) that the term of these acts of consecration, at first blush, is a human person. In truth, Mary is **not** "the absolute term" of these acts. Every act of consecration to serve Mary and to imitate her seeks — through her — more closely and more deeply to serve and to imitate the Lord Jesus himself.

4. The personal consecrations made to the Heart of Jesus and the Heart of Mary take these Hearts as points of reference for more fully fulfilling, in life, the baptismal consecration. This implies that a person commits himself/herself to considering, venerating, and thus, under the impulse of grateful love, imitating *the inner life of Jesus and the inner life of Mary* which the word "Heart" really means. "Learn from me, for I am meek and humble of heart" (Mk 11:29; St. Ambrose in *De virginibus*, 2:7) applies this text to Mary). Further, this implies that such a person hopes to receive grace to live in this way of holiness through the intercession of Jesus and of Mary, and this intercession itself comes forth from their Hearts.

5.1 We cannot demand that the structures of the spiritual life should correspond, in all rigour, exactly and strictly with the harmony and balance of the total complex of the Christian faith. Often enough, it is really impossible to demand this total balance from popular piety.

5.2 However, we should try to have the mystery of salvation, in which Mary is closely associated with Christ her Son, reverberate "correctly" in the spiritual life. This means that we must make the effort to have the consecration to the Heart of Mary understood in such a way, and explicitly expressed in such a way that it is seen as *the way by which a person ultimately consecrates himself/herself to Christ.* For the imitation of Christ, and in fact, *the imitation of his inner life*, is the ultimate term (even if a never fully-attainable term) of the spiritual life. (This has been understood thus from the beginnings of Christianity).

5.3 Similarly it is fitting that the consecration to the Heart of Jesus should be joined with the consecration to the Immaculate Heart of Mary. Thus, a person who begins with one of two Hearts always really consecrates himself/herself to both Hearts. This linking-up reflects the indivisible Alliance which truly exists between the Heart of Jesus and the Heart of Mary.

6.1 The words of Jesus, "And I sanctify myself for them, so that they too may be sanctified in truth" (Jn 17:19) illuminate the meaning of collective consecrations, even the consecration of the entire world, to the Hearts of Jesus and Mary.

6.2 The person who pronounces the act of consecration, consecrates himself/herself, that is, he/she commits himself/herself to live *a life which imitates "the inner states" of these two Hearts.* He/she also entrusts all those referred to and included within the formula of consecration to the protection of the Heart of Jesus and/ or the Heart of Mary (cf. John Paul II, the Act of consecration/ entrustment of the entire world to the Immaculate Heart of Mary, 13 May, 1982).

6.3 Thus can we understand the desire of the Holy Father that as many faithful as possible should join him in making these acts of consecration so that they may all join him in begging for the ever more efficacious help of the Hearts of Jesus and Mary. The very fact that the Roman Pontiffs have placed the entire world under the protection not only of the Sacred Heart (Leo XIII and Pius XI), but also under the protection of the Heart of Mary (Pius XI, Paul VI, and John Paul II), once again shows us clearly the intimate union which binds the Hearts of Jesus and Mary together.

Fatima, Portugal, 19 September, 1986.

Appendix I

Pope John Paul II's Act of Consecration, 13 May, 1982

"For God so loved the world that he gave his only Son, that whoever believes in him should not perish but have eternal life" (Jn 3:16).

It was precisely by reason of this love that the Son of God consecrated himself for all mankind. "And for their sake I consecrate myself, that they also may be consecrated in truth" (Jn 17:19).

By means of that consecration the disciples of all ages are called to spend themselves for the salvation of the world, and to supplement Christ's afflictions for the sake of his Body, that is the Church (cf. 2 Cor 12:15; Col 1:24).

Before you, Mother of Christ, before your Immaculate Heart, I, today, together with the whole Church, unite myself with our Redeemer in this his consecration for the world and for people, which only in his divine Heart has the power to obtain pardon and to secure reparation.

The power of this consecration lasts for all time and embraces all individuals, peoples, and nations. It overcomes every evil that the spirit of darkness is able to awaken, and has in fact awakened in our times, in the heart of man and in his history.

The Church, the Mystical Body of Christ, unites herself, through the service of Peter's successor, to this consecration of our Redeemer...

Hail to you who are wholly united to the redeeming consecration of your Son.

Mother of the Church! Enlighten the People of God along the paths of faith, of hope and love! Help us to live with the whole truth of the consecration of Christ for the entire human family of the modern world.[1]

In entrusting to you, O Mother, the world, all individuals and peoples we also entrust to you the consecration itself, for the world's sake, placing it in your motherly Heart.[2]

---

[1] ORE 1982, 715:12.
[2] *Ibid.*

The Alliance of the Hearts of Jesus and Mary: Hope for the World

Appendix II

The Problem of Consecration

"We have seen that the sometimes vexing and occasionally heated debate over the terminology of 'consecration' as opposed to 'entrustment' does not seem to be envisioned as a matter of opposition in the thought of the Pope (John Paul II), but rather that he employs both terms as well as many others to draw out the various nuances of what it means to belong to Mary."[1]

Thus Fr. Arthur Calkins adverts to a topic which has been unduly magnified by some writers since the Council. As this specialist in papal thought points out the classic definition of consecration to Mary was given by Pius XII, "the total gift of oneself (to Mary) for life and for eternity."[2]

It is suggested that to speak of Catholics "consecrating" themselves is unjustified, as this act was possible only to Christ. We are informed that our separated brethren, Protestants in this case, may be offended by apparent confusion. I think that I may speak with some experience of, and respect for the Protestant mentality. I have Protestant relatives, have had over the years close Protestant friends. I have conducted dialogue with Protestants twenty years before Vatican II and been a member of the Ecumenical Society of the Blessed Virgin Mary since it was introduced to Ireland, participating actively in the International Conference held in the College where I worked in 1984. I served on a joint investigating commission established to study doctrinal and devotional attitudes to Our Lady in the Catholic, Anglican, Presbyterian and Methodist communions in my country.

---

[1] *Totus Tuus*, Academy of the Immaculate, Valatie, New York, 1992, p. 260; the second title of the book is *John Paul II's Program of Consecration and Entrustment*, an exhaustive treatment.

[2] Pius XII, allocution to representatives of the Marian Congregations, 21 January, 1945; cf. Domenico Bertetto, *Il Magisterio Mariano di Pio XII*, Rome, 1956, no. 136; Our Lady, Papal Teachings, Boston, 1961, no. 389; cf. A. Calkins, *op.cit.*, pp. 142, 260.

I see no reason why one should abandon the word 'consecration,' which would mean grave doubt on the use of the word in messages received by certain key figures in the worldwide mission of the Church. It was after the act of consecration at Notre Dame de Victoires that the evangelization of Africa took off, with what magnificent results we know. It was after the consecration of Russia to the Immaculate Heart of Mary that the continuing religious revival really assumed impressive proportions.

Consecration has a fully ecclesial character, through the official papal acts and the spontaneous support of the faithful. This commits our faith. Analogy supports use of the word by the Word made flesh and the members of the Church. In his case it is *ontologically* grounded; in theirs a justifiable act of *moral* choice. If the word "entrustment" (Italian *affidamento*) is used, the usage should not be taken as casting doubt on "consecration."

Appendix III

Mary and the Holy Spirit — Three Saints

St. John Eudes

"The Holy Spirit is the consummation and accomplishment of the adorable mystery of the Holy Trinity. The Heart of the Mother of God is the consummation, the summary and the perfection of all the works of the Holy Trinity in purely created reality, since in contains all that is great, all that is rare in all creatures. For this reason, we can say with Hesychius, Bishop of Jerusalem, that it is *complementum Trinitatis* (*Sermo de Laudibus B. Mariae*) the accomplishment of the Most Holy Trinity, and, as we have already seen, it contributed with the Father, the Son and the Holy Spirit to produce the Godmen by the mystery of the Incarnation. In this work all the power, wisdom, goodness and all other perfections of the Deity must have been used, and as it were, exhausted, since God can do nothing greater.

"The Holy Spirit has been sent into the world to light the darkness, to kindle the fire of divine love in hearts, to accomplish what is lacking in the works, the sufferings and the Passion of the Son of God, and in all his mysteries. What is waiting? That the fruit be applied to souls. But the Heart of the Mother of God is a sun which sheds its light and its fire on all the world. And the very ardent desire it has that the Son of God should not be denied the effects of his designs, and all that he did and suffered in this world for the salvation of humankind should not be in vain and useless, compels this Heart to busy itself incessantly so as to procure, in every possible manner, that the fruit should be applied to our souls."[1]

---

[1] Le Coeur admirable de Marie, 1681, Bk. V, ch. 12.

St. Louis Marie Grignion de Montfort

"God the Holy Spirit, who does not produce any divine Person, became fruitful through Mary, whom he espoused. It was in her, with her, and of her, that he produced his masterpiece, God-made-man, and that he produces every day until the end of the world the members of the body of this adorable Head. For this reason, the more he finds Mary, his dear and inseparable Spouse in a soul, the more powerful and effective he becomes in producing Jesus Christ in that soul and that soul in Jesus Christ. This does not mean that the Blessed Virgin confers on the Holy Spirit a fruitfulness he does not already possess....But it does mean that the Holy Spirit chose to make use of Our Blessed Lady, although he had no absolute need of her, in order to become actively fruitful in producing Jesus Christ and his members in her and by her."[1]

"God the Son has communicated to his Mother all that he has gained by his life and his death, his infinite merits and his admirable virtues, and he has made her the disburser of all that his Father has given him as his inheritance. It is through her that he applies his merits to his members, communicates to them his virtues and distributes to them his graces; she is his mysterious channel, his splendid aqueduct, by which he pours forth his mercies, sweetly and abundantly upon us.

"To his faithful Spouse, Mary, the Holy Spirit has communicated his ineffable gifts, and he has chosen her to be the dispenser of all that he possesses, so that she distributes to whom she wishes, as she wishes, and when she wishes, all his gifts and graces, he himself making no heavenly gift to men except by her virginal hands. This is in accordance with the will of God, who has deigned that we should have all things in Mary."[2]

Here we certainly have a theological insight that is in perfect harmony with the Alliance of the two Hearts.

---

[1] *Treatise on the True Devotion to the Blessed Virgin.* ch. I, article 1.
[2] *Ibid.*, article 2.

St. Maximilian Kolbe

"And what about the Holy Spirit?

"He is in the Immaculate, as the Second Person of the Holy Trinity, the Son of God, is in Jesus, but with this difference: that in Jesus there are two natures, divine and human, in one single Person, the divine Person. The nature and the person of the Immaculate, on the contrary, are distinct from the nature and person of the Holy Spirit. But this union is so inexpressible and perfect that the Holy Spirit acts only through the immaculate, his spouse. Consequently, she is the Mediatress of all the graces of the Holy Spirit. Since every grace is a gift of God the Father through the Son and the Holy Spirit, it follows that there is no grace that does not belong to the Immaculate, which is not offered to her and which does not remain at her free disposal.

"So when we venerate the Immaculate, we venerate the Holy Spirit in a very special manner, and because grace comes from the Father to us through the Son and the Holy Spirit, so, as is only right, the fruits of this grace arise from us to the Father in the reverse order: through the Holy Spirit and the Son, which means through the Immaculate and Jesus."

Apud A. Calkins, *op.cit.*, p. 288.

———

Appendix IV

A Gospel Problem

In studying the Gospels, we meet an apparent difficulty. Especially in the Gospel of John, it is to the Father that Jesus refers his words and deeds: of the Father he says, "I declare to the world what I have heard from him ... I do nothing on my own authority but speak thus, as the Father taught me ... I always do what is pleasing to him ... I came not of my own accord, but he sent me ... it is my Father who glorifies me ... do you say of him whom the Father consecrated and sent into the world, 'You are blaspheming' because I said I am the Son of God?" (Jn 8:26,28,29,42,54; 10:36).

Here Jesus was speaking to the Jews around him. They would not have understood any reference to the Holy Spirit; he had to deal with them on the stock of ideas, not fully developed, which they had. To his disciples in his last encounter with them, he still speaks of the Father, 'He who has seen me has seen my Father. . .Believe me that I am in the Father and the Father in me" (Jn 14:9,11). There is much more besides.

But now he can speak of the Spirit: "And I will pray to the Father, and he will give you another Counselor, to be with you forever, even the Spirit of truth, whom the world cannot receive, because it neither sees him not knows him; you know him, for he dwells with you, and will be in you ... But the Counselor, the Holy Spirit, whom the Father will send in my name, he will teach you all things, and bring to your remembrance all that I have said to you. . . . But when the Counselor comes, whom I will send to you from my Father, even the Spirit of truth who proceeds from the Father, he will bear witness to me ... When the Spirit of truth comes, he will guide you into all the truth ... he will declare to you the things that are to come ... He will glorify me, for he will take what is mine and declare it to you. All that the Father has is mine; therefore I said that he will take what is mine and declare it to you" (Jn 14:16,17,26; 15:26; 16:13,14,15).

As the Gifts of the Spirit proved fruitful in the life of Jesus they were also operative in the thought, feeling, and activity of his

Blessed Mother. If we sinners pride ourselves on receiving the Gifts with their challenge to our outlook and conduct, how much more did she a sinless one! Thus the Spirit active in Jesus and Mary could effect that which he loves, unity. Not a merely passive unity, but dynamic, a mutual communion so wonderfully displayed at Cana, reaching its peak of perfection in the joint sacrifice on Calvary, the playing out, in the presence of the Son bleeding to death, of Simeon's word, inspired by the Spirit on the sword that would pierce the Mother's Heart.

We are at the beginning of the paschal mystery. It will be consummated in the Resurrection, thus described by St. Paul: "If the Spirit of him who raised Jesus from the dead dwells in you, he who raised Christ Jesus from the dead will give life to your mortal bodies also through the Spirit who dwells in you" (Rom 8:11). The first thus raised, who may not have passed through death was, as we know from the dogma of the Assumption, the Mother. Two bodies in glory were the achievement of the Spirit. The bond between them, the profound unity begun in the moment of the Annunciation was now totally sealed to the glory of the Holy Trinity and for our salvation.

Here then is the true source of the unity of the two Hearts which has been increasingly taught by saints and servants of the Lord. It was the Spirit who, by his all-powerful intervention created the Heart of Christ beside that of Mary, whom he had made immaculate in the first moment of her existence, joining them in the same blood stream; he finally assured the consummation of his work by raising Son and Mother to indestructible life; thus they are linked in glory coming to both from him, uniting them in his power.

The same passage of the Epistle to the Romans gives us also the answer to what seemed a problem, Christ's insistence on his relationship with the Father. "For all who are led by the Spirit of God are sons of God. For you did not receive the spirit of slavery to fall back into fear, but you have received the spirit of sonship. When we cry 'Abba! Father!' it is the Spirit himself bearing witness with our spirit that we are children of God, and if children, then heirs, heirs of God and fellow heirs with Christ, provided we suffer with him in order that we also be glorified with him" (Rom 8:14-17).

Bearing in min what John Paul II said about the Spirit in the life of Christ, may we not conclude that it was the Spirit who in Jesus prompted him so speak of, and to, the Father, notably in the priestly prayer in John XVII, the sublime, poignant, profound self-statement of God the Redeemer.